Piano Book for Kids 5 & Up

No Music Reading Required

Damon Ferrante

Learn to Play Famous Piano Songs, Easy Pieces & Fun Music, Piano Technique, Music Theory & How to Read Music (Book & Streaming Video Lessons)

Introduction: How the Book & Videos Work

As a piano professor and piano teacher for over twenty five years, I have wanted to help young, beginner piano students succeed and be excited about playing famous and beautiful piano music. In the past, beginner piano books for children have taken a rather dull and uninspiring approach. Most of the time these books just throw together songs and techniques in a random and confusing way; sometimes these books are no better than blurry photocopies.

This book and video course takes a new and innovative approach!

Piano Book for Kids 5 & Up makes learning famous piano pieces fun, easy, interactive, and engaging. The book and streaming videos follow a step-by-step lesson format for learning some of the most famous music: pieces that are wonderful for children to play for themselves, family, and friends!

In *Piano Book for Kids 5 & Up,* each lesson builds on the previous one in a clear and easy-to-understand manner. No music reading is necessary. I walk the young reader through how to play these wonderful pieces, starting with very easy music, at the beginning of the book, and advancing, little by little, as the child masters new repertoire and techniques. As the young student is able to play these new pieces, he or she will also greatly improve his or her abilities on the piano! Along the way, the child will learn to read music, play chords, learn rhythms, techniques, and music theory. There are some silly jokes interspersed throughout the book, as well!

The Videos

This symbol means that there is a video lesson that corresponds to the material presented on the lesson page. These video lessons cover the concepts presented and also give instruction and tips on how to play certain famous pieces from the book.

To access the video lessons, go to steeplechasemusic.com and click on the link at the top of the page for Piano Books. Then, from the Piano Books webpage, click on the image for this book, "Piano Book for Kids 5 & Up". On the webpage for the *Piano Book for Kids 5 & Up*, you will see a link to Video Lessons. Click that link for the Video Lessons webpage for this book. The video lessons are free and there is no limit on the number of times you may watch them.

Table of Contents

Page:

Table of Contents for the Video Lessons

Important!

To access the video lessons, go to steeplechasemusic.com and click on the link at the top of the page for Piano Books. Then, from the Piano Books webpage, click on the image for this book, "Piano Book for Kids 5 & Up". On the webpage for the *Piano Book for Kids 5 & Up*, you will see a link to Video Lessons. Click that link for the Video Lessons webpage for this book. The video lessons are free and there is no limit on the number of times you may watch them.

Steeplechase Music Books

Also by Damon Ferrante

Piano Scales, Chords & Arpeggios Lessons with Elements of Basic Music Theory: Fun, Step-By-Step Guide for Beginner to Advanced Levels (Book & Videos)

Guitar Adventures: Fun, Step-By-Step Guide to Beginner Guitar (Book & Videos)

Beginner Piano Book for Adults: Teach Yourself How to Play Famous Piano Songs, Read Music, Theory & Technique (Book & Streaming Video Lessons)

Guitar Adventures for Kids: Fun, Step-By-Step, Beginner Lesson Guide to Get You Started (Book & Videos)

Beginner Rock Guitar Lessons: Instruction Guide (Book & Videos)

Beginner Classical Piano Music: Teach Yourself How to Play Famous Piano Pieces by Bach, Mozart, Beethoven and the Great Composers (Book, Streaming Videos & MP3 Audio)

Piano Book for Kids 5 & Up - Beginner Level: Learn to Play Famous Piano Songs, Easy Pieces & Fun Music, Piano Technique, Music Theory & How to Read Music (Book & Streaming Video Lessons)

by Damon Ferrante

For additional information about
music books, recordings, and concerts,
please visit the Steeplechase website:
www.steeplechasemusic.com

ISBN-13: 978-0692115626 (Steeplechase Arts)
ISBN-10: 0692115625

Getting Started: Introduction & Basic Music Concepts

Finding the Black & White Keys on the Piano

> - Do you see that the piano is made up of black keys and white keys?
> - Can you point to the white keys on your piano keyboard?
> - Can you point to the black keys on your piano keyboard?
> - Try playing some of the white keys and the black keys.

Are there any green keys on the piano?

Here are some black keys.

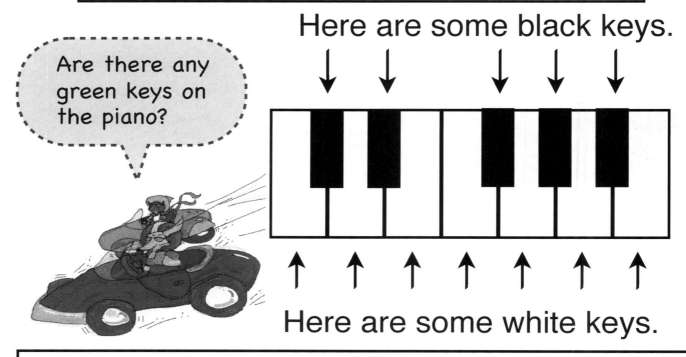

Here are some white keys.

> - Do you see that the black keys are in groups of two and three?
> - Try putting your pointer and middle fingers on a group of two black keys.
> - *Great job!*
> - Now, try putting your pointer, middle, and ring fingers on a group of three black keys.

3 Black Keys   2 Black Keys   3 Black Keys

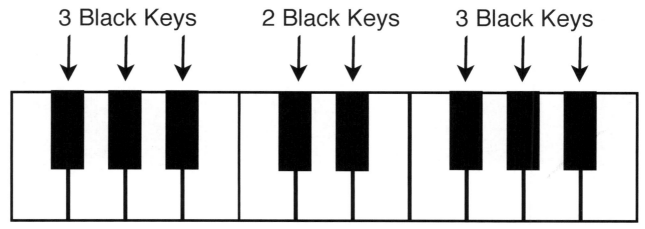

Learning the Keyboard Notes

- The White Keys on the piano follow a pattern like the alphabet. This pattern goes from A to G. In other words, the pattern goes like this: A, B, C, D, E, F, G.
- The pattern starts at the bottom (low bass notes) of the piano keyboard and repeats many times as the notes go upward and get higher in pitch ("sound").
- The lowest key on the piano is the note "A".
- Can you find the lowest key (the note "A") on your piano and play it?
- What does it sound like? Some people say it sounds like a growling lion.

Down
(Lower Pitch)   ←——————→   Up
(Higher Pitch)

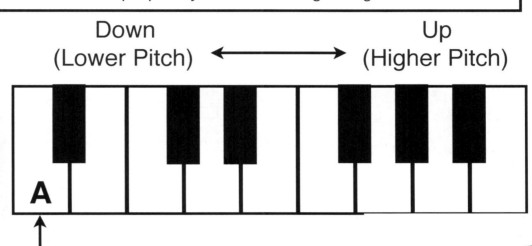

A

Check out video 1

This is the note "A".
It is the lowest note on the piano

Try playing the low A key with your right-hand thumb.

- Try playing the low A with your right hand pointer.
- Try playing the low A with your right hand middle finger.
- Try playing the low A with your right hand ring finger.
- Try playing the low A with your right hand pinky.

- Now, try playing the low A with your left hand thumb.
- Try playing the low A with your left hand pointer.
- Try playing the low A with your left hand middle finger.
- Try playing the low A with your left hand ring finger.
- Try playing the low A with your left hand pinky.

Learning the Order of the Keys

- Do you remember that we said that the White Keys on the piano follow a pattern like the alphabet? The pattern goes like this: A, B, C, D, E, F, G.
- Let's pretend that the letter of each key on the piano is linked with a type of food.
- For example, let's image that the piano keyboard is a picnic table with food on it. The food, on this "pretend table", will be placed in a set order going from left to right (See the chart below).

The White Keys:
A= Apple
B= Banana
C= Cheese
D= Dessert
E= Eggs
F= Fish
G= Grapes

Down
(Lower Pitch) ←————→ Up
(Higher Pitch)

This is the note "A". It is the lowest note on the piano

- Let's find that low "A" key on the piano and play it. The key A is "A" for "apple".
- Let's play the A again and say "apple". This way, we will link the key and it's place on the piano keyboard with an image, in this case, an apple.
- Let's go up to the next key to the right and and play the B and say "banana".
  (If we go to the left from the low "A" key, we will run out of keys on the piano. Ha!).
- Now, let's keep going up the keyboard and playing the notes and saying the words. For example, "C" for cheese, "D" for dessert, and so on. The whole pattern will be this: Apple, Banana, Cheese, Dessert, Eggs, Fish, Grapes. The pattern will repeat after "G" for grapes.

 Joke Time! "Knock, Knock." "Who's There?" "Lettuce"."
"Lettuce, who?" "Let us in; it's lunchtime." Ha! Ha!

Finding Our Way Around on the Piano Keyboard

- Let's go back to our imaginary picnic table from the previous page.
- Let's continue to imagine that the piano keyboard is a picnic table.
- Do you see that there are groups of two black keys and groups of three black keys on the keyboard of the piano?
- Now, let's pretend that the groups of two black keys are each two juice boxes.
- Let's also pretend that the groups of three black keys are napkins.
- Can you find a group of two black keys (or "juice boxes") near the middle of the piano?

Hey, are you going to drink those juice boxes?

D

The note D for dessert.

- The white key in between the "two juice boxes" (black keys) is the note D.
- Can you find the D and play it? Can you find other Ds up and down the keyboard? (Hint: Look for the white key between a set of "two juice boxes".)

Hand Position & Finger Number

- To create a good hand position for piano playing is easy. With both hands, imagine that you are holding an apple (with your palms facing upward and your fingers curved). Then, turn your palms to the floor and keep your fingers curved.
- For piano playing, our fingers are given numbers. The numbers are the same for both hands.

Check out video 1

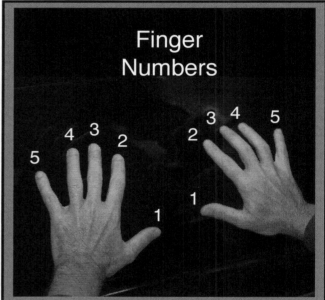

- RH stands for Right Hand.
- LH stands for Left Hand.

Finger Numbers
- Thumb = Finger #1
- Pointer = Finger #2
- Middle = Finger #3
- Ring = Finger #4
- Pinky = Finger #5

The finger numbers are the same for both hands. For example, the thumb is finger #1 in both the right hand and left hand and the pinky is finger #5 in both hands.

Finding Middle C
& Good Posture at the Piano

- So far, one of the things that we have learned is that the black keys are in groups of two and three keys.
- If you look near the middle of the piano keyboard, you will see a set of two black keys (or "juice boxes" Ha!). The white key directly to the left of this set of two black keys (near the middle of the piano keyboard) is called "Middle C".
- Middle C is an important note on the piano. We will be playing it in many of our songs. For some help in locating Middle C on the piano, see video lesson 1.

Check out video 1

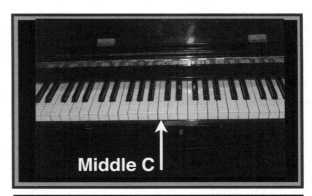

Middle C

From the beginning of your piano playing, it is important to practice good posture: keep your back straight and your arms and shoulders relaxed.

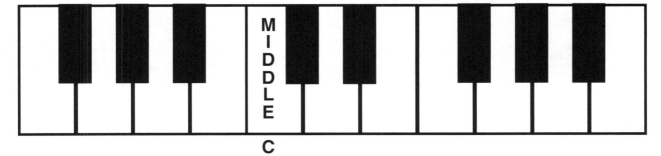

M I D D L E C

Exercises:
- Try Locating Middle C with Finger #1 (Thumb) of your Right Hand (RH)
- Try Locating Middle C with Finger #1 (Thumb) of your Left Hand (LH)

Right Hand

Wizards: A Three-Note Song, Using the Right Hand ("RH")

- Try this song, *Wizards*, which use the notes C, D, and E in the right hand ("RH").
- In your right hand, use Thumb for Middle C, use Pointer for D, and use Middle Finger for E.
- Take a look at the keyboard chart and photo below and practice the song 5-10 times.
- As an extra bonus, try saying the letter names aloud as you play the song. This will help you associate the note name with the key and finger number.

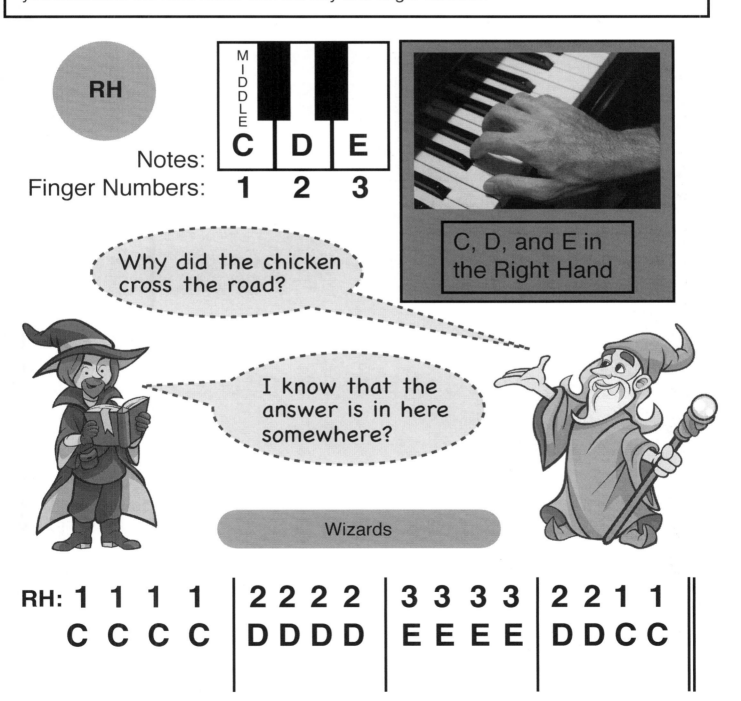

C, D, and E in the Right Hand

15

Mountain Sunrise:
A Three-Note Song,
Using the Right Hand ("RH")

- Let's play this new song, *Mountain Sunrise.* which uses the notes C, D, and E in the right hand ("RH").
- Use Thumb for Middle C, use Pointer for D, and use Middle Finger for E.
- To refresh your memory on the location of the keys, take a look at the keyboard chart and photo from the previous page. Practice the song 5-10 times.

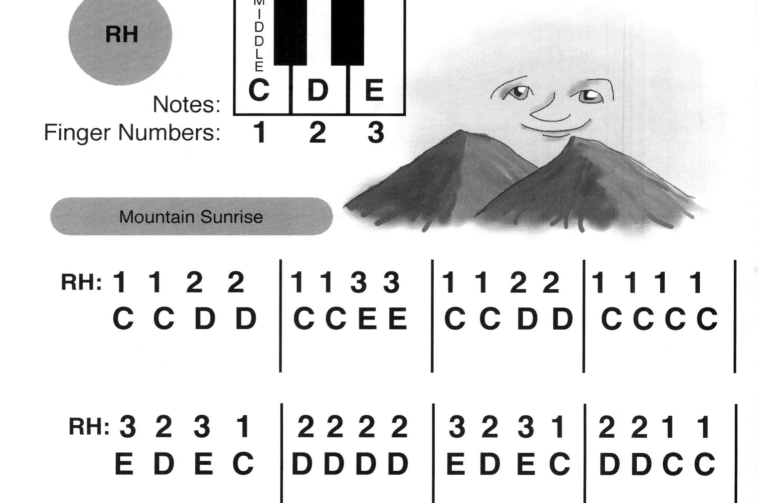

Mountain Sunrise

RH: **1 1 2 2** | **1 1 3 3** | **1 1 2 2** | **1 1 1 1**
C C D D | **C C E E** | **C C D D** | **C C C C**

RH: **3 2 3 1** | **2 2 2 2** | **3 2 3 1** | **2 2 1 1**
E D E C | **D D D D** | **E D E C** | **D D C C**

RH: **1 1 2 2** | **1 1 3 3** | **1 1 2 2** | **1 1 1 1**
C C D D | **C C E E** | **C C D D** | **C C C C**

Soccer Fun: A Three-Note Song Using the Right Hand

- Try this song, which also uses the notes C, D, and E in the right hand ("RH").

RH

MIDDLE

Notes: **C D E**

Finger Numbers: **1 2 3**

Try saying the notes aloud as you play each song.

Soccer Fun

RH: **2 2 1 1** | **2 2 3 3** | **2 2 1 2** | **2 2 1 2** |
D D C C | **D D E E** | **D D C D** | **D D C D** |

RH: **3 2 3 1** | **2 2 2 2** | **3 2 3 1** | **2 2 1 1** |
E D E C | **D D D D** | **E D E C** | **D D C C** |

The double lines (called the "Double Bar") indicate the end of a song or piece.

RH: **1 1 3 3** | **2 2 3 3** | **1 1 3 3** | **2 2 1 1** ‖
C C E E | **D D E E** | **C C E E** | **D D C C**

Counting & Measures

- Music is made up of groups of beats called measures.
- These measures are set off by vertical lines, called "bar lines".
- Measures most commonly contain 2, 3, or 4 beats.
- Below, are examples of sets of four measures in 4/4 time.
- In 4/4 time, you will count 4 beats for each measure.
  In other words, you will count: 1234, 1234, 1234, 1234.
- Try counting aloud and clapping the beats for the exercise below.

 Check out video 2

Example 1:

| 1 2 3 4 | 1 2 3 4 | 1 2 3 4 | 1 2 3 4 |

Example 2:
Try Clapping on the X: On the First Beat.

| 1 2 3 4 | 1 2 3 4 | 1 2 3 4 | 1 2 3 4 |
| X | X | X | X |

Example 3:
Try Clapping on the X: On the First and Third Beats.

| 1 2 3 4 | 1 2 3 4 | 1 2 3 4 | 1 2 3 4 |
| X X | X X | X X | X X |

Example 4:
Try Clapping on the X: On the Second Beat.

| 1 2 3 4 | 1 2 3 4 | 1 2 3 4 | 1 2 3 4 |
| X | X | X | X |

Sailboats: Counting along with a Three-Note Song (RH)

- Try counting aloud (1234) for each measure, while playing this song.
- The song uses the notes C, D, and E in the right hand ("RH"): Fingers 1, 2, and 3. *Have fun!*

RH

Notes:
Finger Numbers:

C	D	E
1	2	3

Sailboats

*The Numbers in these songs are for the <u>Beats</u>, <u>not</u> the Finger Numbers.

Beats: **1** 2 3 4 | 1 2 3 4 | 1 2 3 4 | 1 2 3 4
D D C D | D D C D | E E D D | E E D D

Beats: **1** 2 3 4 | 1 2 3 4 | 1 2 3 4 | 1 2 3 4
C C C C | D D D D | E E D D | C C C C

Beats: **1** 2 3 4 | 1 2 3 4 | 1 2 3 4 | 1 2 3 4
E D C C | D D E E | D D C D | E D C C

19

Mary's Lamb & Jingle Bells: Five-Note Songs

- Let's add 2 new notes for the right hand ("RH"): F and G.
- F will be played with the 4th finger (Ring Finger).
- G will be played with the 5th finger (Pinky Finger).

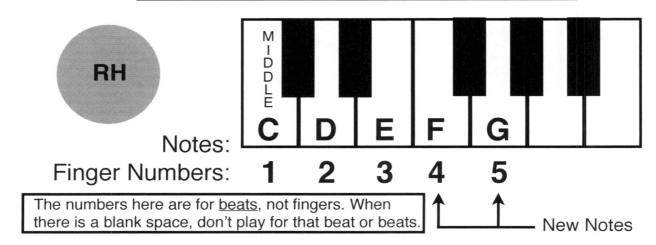

RH

Notes: C   D   E   F   G

Finger Numbers: **1**   **2**   **3**   **4**   **5**

The numbers here are for <u>beats</u>, not fingers. When there is a blank space, don't play for that beat or beats.

New Notes

Mary's Little Lamb

Beats: **1** **2** **3** **4**	**1 2 3 4**	**1 2 3 4**	**1 2 3 4**
E D C D	E E E	D D D	E G G
Ma- ry had a	lit- tle lamb,	lit- tle lamb,	lit- tle lamb.

Jingle Bells

Beats: **1** **2** **3** **4**	**1 2 3 4**	**1 2 3 4**	**1 2 3 4**
E E E	E E E	E G C D	E
Jin- gle Bells,	Jin- gle Bells,	Jin- gle all the	way.

Beats: **1** **2** **3** **4**	**1 2 3 4**	**1 2 3 4**	**1 2 3 4**
F F F F	F E E E	E D D E	D G
Oh! What fun it	is to ride in	a one-horse open	sleigh! Hey!

Beethoven's Ode to Joy: A Five-Note Song for the Right Hand

- Here is a famous song that uses the five fingers of the right hand: *Ode to Joy.*
- Beethoven wrote this great melody for his *Ninth Symphony.*
- Remember to find Middle C with the Thumb of your right hand (RH).

Notes:

Finger Numbers: **1   2   3   4   5**

The numbers here are for <u>beats</u>, not fingers. When there is a blank space, don't play for that beat or beats.

New Notes

Ode to Joy

Beats:	1 2 3 4	1 2 3 4	1 2 3 4	1 2 3 4
	E E F G	G F E D	C C D E	E D D

Beats:	1 2 3 4	1 2 3 4	1 2 3 4	1 2 3 4
	E E F G	G F E D	C C D E	D C C

21

Left Hand

In Winter:
A Three-Note Song for the Left

- Try this song, which uses the notes A, B, and Middle C in the left hand ("LH").
- In your left hand, use Thumb for Middle C, use Pointer for B, and use Middle Finger for A.
- Take a look at the keyboard chart and photo below and practice the song 5-10 times.
- As an extra bonus, try saying the letter names aloud as you play the song. This will help you associate the note name with the key and finger number. ***Have Fun!***

A, B, and C in the Left Hand

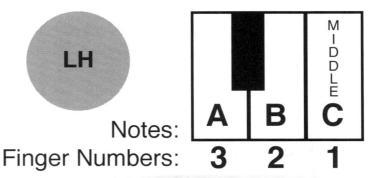

LH

Notes:

A	B	C (MIDDLE)

Finger Numbers: 3   2   1

In Winter

The numbers here are for <u>fingers</u>, not beats.

LH: 1 1 2 3 | 1 1 2 3 | 2 2 3 3 | 2 2 3 3
      C C B A | C C B A | B B A A | B B A A

LH: 3 2 1 2 | 3 2 1 2 | 1 1 3 3 | 1 2 3 3
      A B C B | A B C B | C C A A | C B A A

Clouds: A Three-Note Song for the Left Hand

Try this song, which also uses the notes A, B, and C in the Left hand

LH

MIDDLE

Notes: A B C
Finger Numbers: 3 2 1

Try saying the notes aloud as you play each song.

Clouds

The numbers here are for <u>fingers</u>, not beats.

LH: **2 3 2 3** | **1 1 1 1** | **2 3 2 3** | **1 1 3 3**
B A B A | **C C C C** | **B A B A** | **C C A A**

LH: **1 3 2 1** | **1 3 2 1** | **2 2 3 3** | **1 2 3 3**
C A B C | **C A B C** | **B B A A** | **C B A A**

LH: **1 3 1 3** | **2 3 2 3** | **1 3 1 3** | **2 2 3 3**
C A C A | **B A B A** | **C A C A** | **B B A A**

 Joke Time! "What did the Teddy Bear say after dinner?"
"No dessert for me; I'm stuffed." Ha! Ha! Ha!

What are Time Signatures?

Check out video 3

- Measures are composed of groups of beats called Time Signatures or Meter (both terms mean the same thing and are interchangeable).
- The most common Time Signatures (or "meters") are groups of 2, 3, or 4 beats per measure: 2/4, 3/4, and 4/4 Time Signatures.
- 2/4 Time Signature groups the notes into measures of 2 beats. Count: "One, Two" for each measure.
- 3/4 Time Signature groups the notes into measures of 3 beats. Count: "One, Two, Three" for each measure.
- 4/4 Time Signature groups the notes into measures of 4 beats. Count: "One, Two, Three, Four" for each measure.
- Below, are examples of sets of four measures in 2/4, 3/4, and 4/4.
- Count aloud and clap on the first beat for the exercises below.

Example 1: 2/4 Time Signature
Try Clapping on the X: On the First Beat.

$\frac{2}{4}$

| 1   2 | 1   2 | 1   2 | 1   2 |
| X | X | X | X |

Example 2: 3/4 Time Signature
Try Clapping on the X: On the First Beat.

$\frac{3}{4}$

| 1 2 3 | 1 2 3 | 1 2 3 | 1 2 3 |
| X | X | X | X |

Example 3: 4/4 Time Signature
Try Clapping on the X: On the First Beat.

$\frac{4}{4}$

| 1 2 3 4 | 1 2 3 4 | 1 2 3 4 | 1 2 3 4 |
| X | X | X | X |

Falling Leaves: Counting along with a Song in 3/4 Time (LH)

- Try counting aloud (123) for each measure, while playing this song.
- The song is in 3/4 Time Signatures (which can also be called "3/4 Time").
- The song uses the notes A, B, and C in the left hand ("LH"): Fingers 3, 2, and 1.
  Have fun!

The Numbers in this song are for the <u>Beats</u>, <u>not</u> the Finger Numbers.

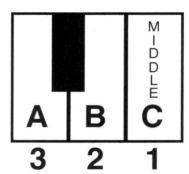

LH

Notes: A B C

MIDDLE

Finger Numbers: 3 2 1

Falling Leaves

Beats:

3/4 | 1 2 3 | 1 2 3 | 1 2 3 | 1 2 3 |
        | C A A | C A A | B A A | C A A |

Beats:

| 1 2 3 | 1 2 3 | 1 2 3 | 1 2 3 |
| A B C | A B C | B A B | C B A |

Beats:

| 1 2 3 | 1 2 3 | 1 2 3 | 1 2 3 |
| C B A | C C C | B B B | C B A |

Sunny Day: A Five-Note Song for the Left Hand (LH)

- Let's add 2 new notes for the left hand ("LH"): F and G.
- F will be played with the 5th finger (Pinky Finger).
- G will be played with the 4th finger (Ring Finger).

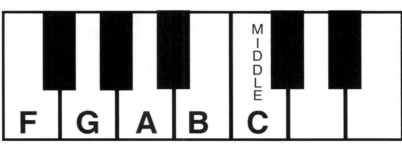

LH

Notes: | **F** | **G** | **A** | **B** | **C** (MIDDLE)

Finger Numbers: **5 4 3 2 1**

New Notes

- This song is in 3/4 time (or "time signature").
- Remember to count like this:
  "One, Two, Three" for each measure.
- The numbers here are for the <u>beats</u>.

Sunny Day

Beats:

3	1	2	3	1	2	3	1	2	3	1	2	3
4	C	A	F	C	A	F	G	G	C	C	A	F

Beats:

1	2	3	1	2	3	1	2	3	1	2	3
F	G	A	F	A	C	F	G	A	C	A	F

Springtime: A Five-Note Song for the Left Hand (LH)

- Here is a song that uses the five fingers of the left hand.
- Remember to find Middle C with the Thumb of your left hand (LH).

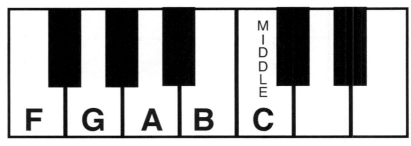

Notes: F G A B C

Finger Numbers: 5 4 3 2 1

This song is in 4/4 time. Remember to count four beats for each measure. The numbers here are for <u>beats</u>, not fingers.

Springtime

Beats:

4 1 2 3 4	1 2 3 4	1 2 3 4	1 2 3 4
4 F G A G	C C G G	F G A G	C B C C

1 2 3 4	1 2 3 4	1 2 3 4	1 2 3 4
C G F G	C G F G	A A C C	G G G G

1 2 3 4	1 2 3 4	1 2 3 4	1 2 3 4
C G F G	C G F G	A A C C	G F F F

28

Both Hands

Three Kings: A Song For Both Hands: A,B,C,D,E

- Now we will start playing songs that use both the right and left hands.
- Find Middle C with both your right- and left-hand thumbs.
- For the next few pieces, both thumbs will share Middle C.
- These first songs will involve 3 fingers for each hand.
- Gradually we will add additional fingers.
- The letters positioned above the beats are for right hand (RH).
- The letters positioned below the beats are for left hand (LH).

Check out video 4

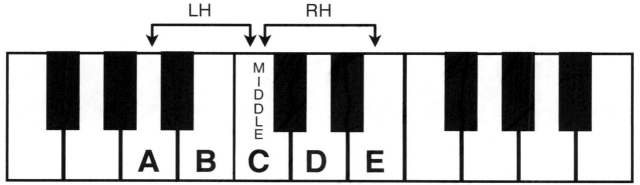

Finger Numbers: **3   2   1   2   3**

Both Thumbs (RH and LH) share Middle C.

*The Numbers in this song are for the <u>Beats</u>, <u>not</u> the Finger Numbers.

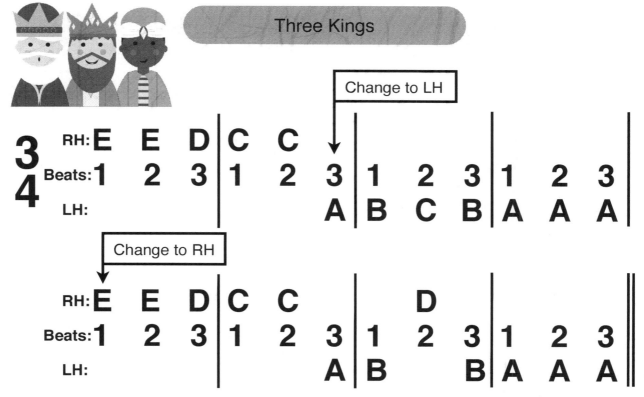

Three Kings

Fifth Symphony & Balloons: Pieces for Both Hands

- Here are 2 pieces for both hands.
- They use the notes A, B, C, D, and E.
- The numbers listed are for the <u>beats</u>, not the finger numbers.
- If there is a blank space, don't play for that beat or beats.
- Both Thumbs will share Middle C.

LH   RH

A   B   C   D   E

Finger Numbers: **3   2   1   2   3**

Both Thumbs (RH and LH) share Middle C.

Beethoven 5th Symphony Theme

$\frac{3}{4}$	RH:	E	E	E	C			D	D	D			
	Beats:	1	2	3	1	2	3	1	2	3	1	2	3
	LH:										B		

Balloons

$\frac{3}{4}$	RH:	C	D	E	C			C	D	E	G		C
	Beats:	1	2	3	1	2	3	1	2	3	1	2	3
	LH:					G	G						G

Yankee Doodle & March: Songs for Both Hands

- Let's add 2 notes: G in the Left Hand and F in the Right Hand.
- Both of these new notes will be played with the Ring Fingers.

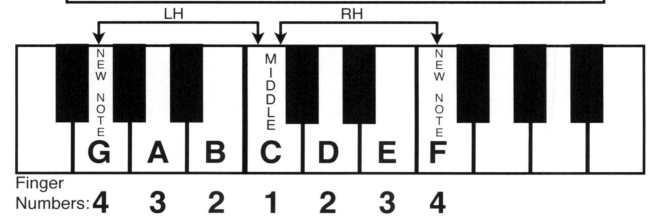

Finger Numbers: **4 3 2 1 2 3 4**

Both Thumbs (RH and LH) share Middle C.

Yankee Doodle

RH:	C	C	D	E		C	E	D			C	C	D	E	C			
Beats:	1	2	3	4		1	2	3	4		1	2	3	4	1	2	3	4
LH:																		B

RH:	C	C	D	E		F	E	D	C						C		C	
Beats:	1	2	3	4		1	2	3	4		1	2	3	4	1	2	3	4
LH:											B	G	A	B				

March

RH:	C		C				C			C		C				C	C	
Beats:	1	2	3	4		1	2	3	4		1	2	3	4	1	2	3	4
LH:		G		G		A	B		G			G		G	A	B		

Twinkle, Twinkle, Little Star
Both Hands: G,A,B,C,D,E,F

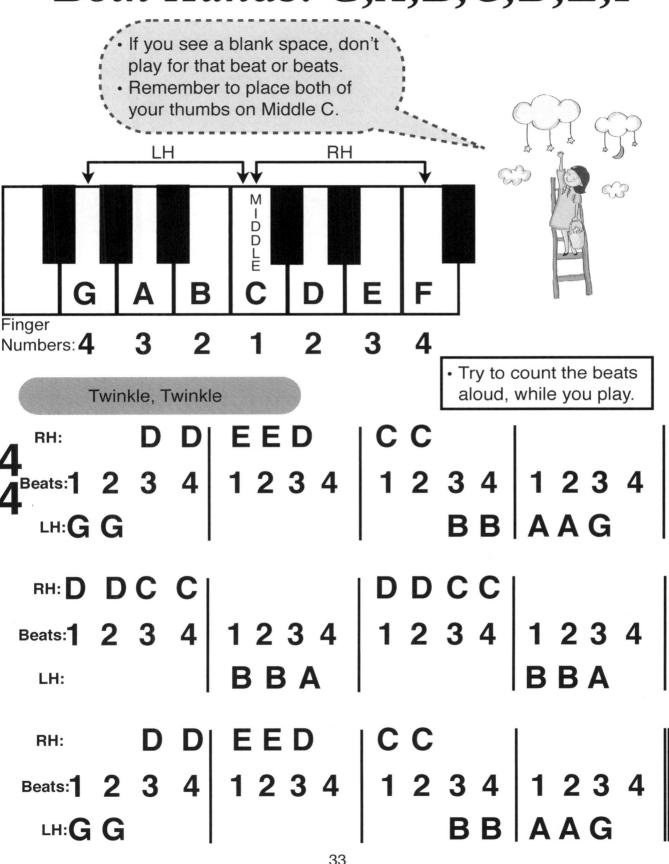

The Ballgame: Both Hands
F,G,A,B,C,D,E,F,G

- Let's add 1 more note for each hand: "F" in the Left Hand and "G" in the right hand.
- Both of these notes ("F" in LH and "G" in RH) will be played with the 5th finger (Pinky).
- Remember, the numbers in these songs are for the <u>beats</u>, not for the fingers.

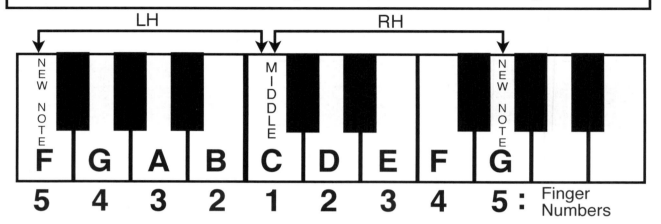

- Both Thumbs (RH and LH) share Middle C for this song.
- If there is a blank space, don't play for that beat or beats. In music, these silent beats are called "Rests. We will learn more about Rests later in this book.
- For "The Ballgame", try to say the note names aloud, as you play the song. This will help you associate the letter names with the keys and will allow you to improve faster.

The Ballgame

RH:			F	D	C		C					
Beats: 1	2	3	1	2	3	1	2	3	1	2	3	
LH: F					A				G			

RH:			F	D	C		C					
Beats: 1	2	3	1	2	3	1	2	3	1	2	3	
LH: F					A				C			

($\frac{3}{4}$ time signature)

Music Theory: What are Intervals?

Check out video 5

- In music, the distance between any 2 notes is called an "Interval".
- Intervals can be played at the same time, for example, if you press down two piano keys or they can be played one after the other, for example, if you play the note "C" and then the note "D".
- On the piano, the easiest way to understand intervals is to look at the keyboard. Play Middle C with your Left-Hand Index Finger, then play D with your Right-Hand Index finger. This interval is called a 2nd.
- Next, play Middle C with your Left-Hand Index Finger, then play E with your Right-Hand Index finger. This interval is called a 3rd.
- Follow these steps in the 2 diagrams below. Use the Left-Hand Index Finger when you see LH and use the Right-Hand Index Finger when you see RH.

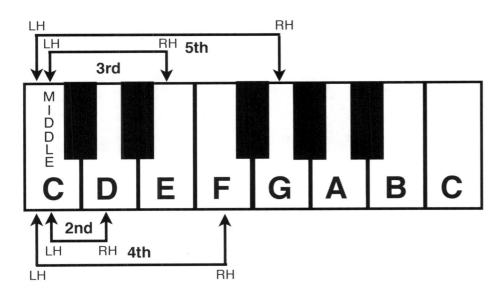

C to D = 2nd
C to E = 3rd
C to F = 4th
C to G = 5th

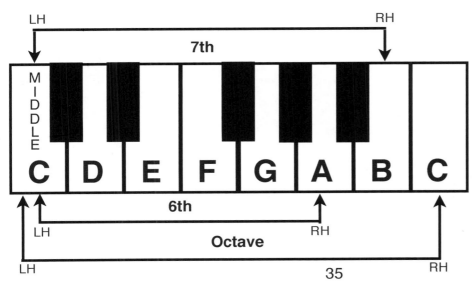

C to A = 6th
C to B = 7th
C to C = Octave

Holiday Fun: Both Hands at the Same Time: F,G,A,B,C,D,E,F,G

- In these next songs, we will be playing notes with the right hand and left hand at the same time.
- When one letter is on top of another letter, play both at the same time. *Have Fun!*

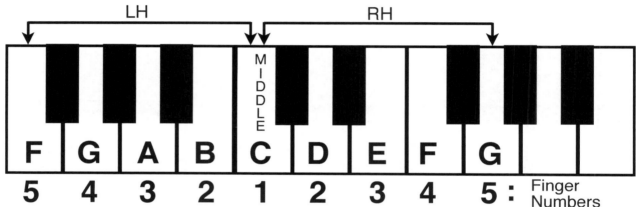

Holiday Fun!

RH:	G	G	G	G	E	E	E	E	F	F	F	F	E	E	E	E
Beats:	1	2	3	4	1	2	3	4	1	2	3	4	1	2	3	4
LH:	C	C	C	C	C	C	C	C	C	C	C	C	C	C	C	C

RH:	G	G	G	G	E	E	E	E	F	F	F	F	C			
Beats:	1	2	3	4	1	2	3	4	1	2	3	4	1	2	3	4
LH:	C	C	C	C	C	C	C	C	C	C	C	C	G			

$\frac{4}{4}$

Love Somebody & Snow Flurries:
Both Hands at the Same Time:
F,G,A,B,C,D,E,F,G

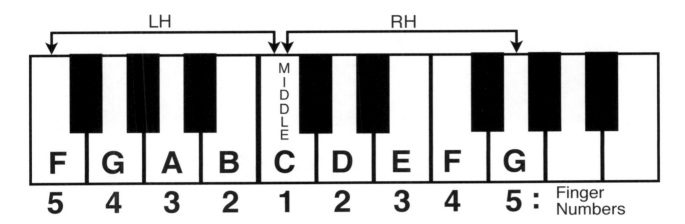

F	G	A	B	C	D	E	F	G	
5	4	3	2	1	2	3	4	5 :	Finger Numbers

Love Somebody

RH:	C E G G	D E F	C E G G	F E D	
4 Beats:	1 2 3 4	1 2 3 4	1 2 3 4	1 2 3 4	
4 LH:	G	G	G	A	

RH:	C E G G	D E F	E E D D	C C C	
Beats:	1 2 3 4	1 2 3 4	1 2 3 4	1 2 3 4	
LH:	G	G	G	G	

Snow Flurries

RH:	E	E	D D D D	C C C C	
4 Beats:	1 2 3 4	1 2 3 4	1 2 3 4	1 2 3 4	
4 LH:	A B C B	A B C B	B B B B	A A A A	

37

Ode to Joy & The Snowman:
Both Hands at the Same Time:
F,G,A,B,C,D,E,F,G

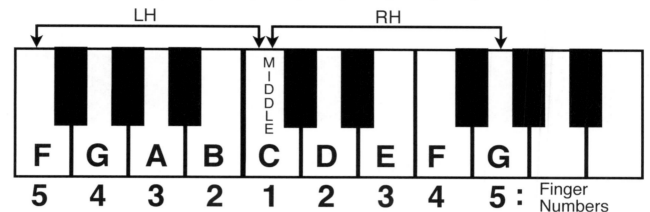

Try this more advanced version of Beethoven's *Ode to Joy.*

Ode to Joy

E	**E**	**F**	**G**	**G**	**F**	**E**	**D**	**C**	**C**	**D**	**E**	**E**	**D**	**D**	

4/4 Beats:
1 2 3 4 | **1 2 3 4** | **1 2 3 4** | **1 2 3 4**

G | **C** | **A** | **G**

| **E** | **E** | **F** | **G** | **G** | **F** | **E** | **D** | **C** | **C** | **D** | **E** | **D** | **C** | **C** | |

1 2 3 4 | **1 2 3 4** | **1 2 3 4** | **1 2 3 4**

G | **C** | **A** | **G**

The Snowman

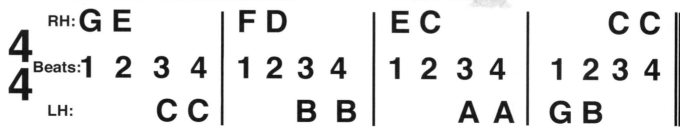

RH: **G E** | **F D** | **E C** | **C C**

4/4 Beats: **1 2 3 4** | **1 2 3 4** | **1 2 3 4** | **1 2 3 4**

LH: **C C** | **B B** | **A A** | **G B**

When the Saints Go Marching In & What are Upbeats

- In music, there are many songs and pieces that use Upbeats.
- An Upbeat (or Upbeats) is a note or group of notes that occur before the first full measure of a song or piece of music.
- Upbeats act as very short introductory phrases that emphasize an important note or word at the beginning of a song. For example, in *When the Saints Go Marching In,* the words "Oh when the" are the upbeat. They lead into and accentuate the word "saints".

These Upbeats Start on Beat 2

Do you notice how both of these phases -- "Oh, When the Saints" and "Go Marching In"-- start on the 2nd Beat? These are Upbeat figures.

$\frac{4}{4}$

1	2	3	4	1	2	3	4	1	2	3	4	1	2	3	4
	Oh,	When	the	Saints					go	March-ing		in.			

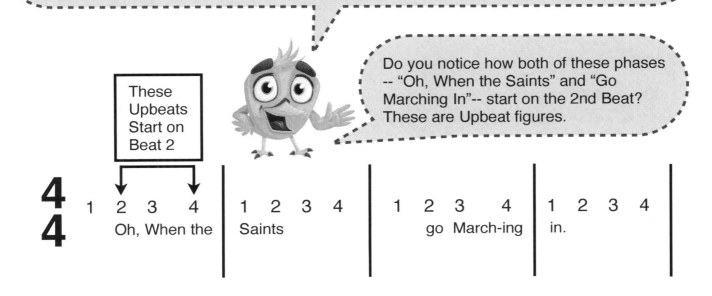

When the Saints Go Marching In

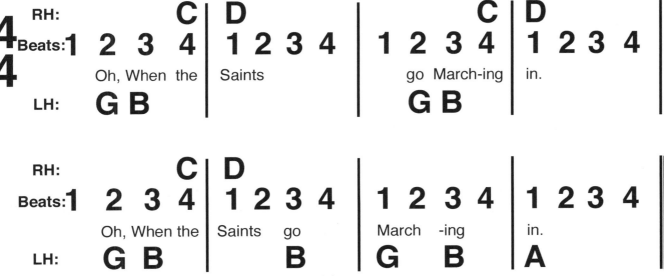

Rhythm & Meter

What Are Whole Notes, Half Notes & Quarter Notes?

- Let's take a look at some basic rhythms.
- Quarter Notes are notes that get 1 Beat (or Count).
- Half Notes are notes that get 2 Beats (or Counts).
- Whole Notes are notes that get 4 Beats (or Counts).
- In the next 3 examples, try counting on each beat of the 4/4 measures aloud, for example: 1,2,3,4.
- Clap on the quarter, half, and whole notes.

♩ = 1 Beat   ♩ = 2 Beats   o = 4 Beats

Check out video 6

Example 1:
Try Clapping on each "X", while counting the beats.

Example 2:
Try Clapping on each "X", while counting the beats.

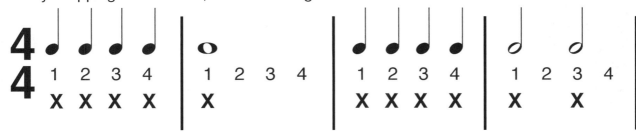

Example 3:
Try Clapping on each "X", while counting the beats.

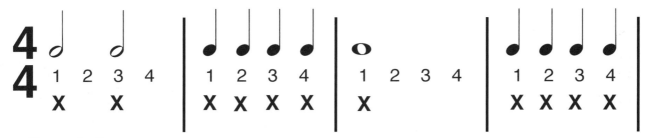

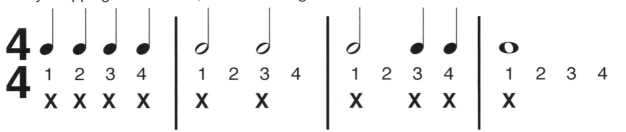

41

On the Beach & The Bells: Songs with Half Notes & Quarter Notes

- Try these songs that use Half Notes (2 beats or counts) and quarter notes (1 beat or count).
- All of the songs on this page are for the Right Hand (RH).
- Try to count aloud (1,2,3,4) for each measure.

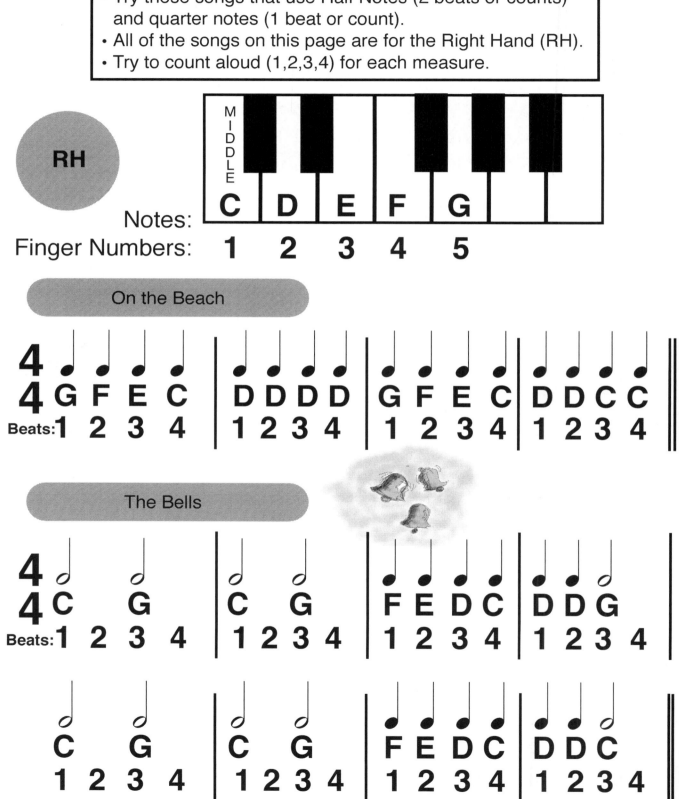

Summer Day: A Five-Note Song with Half Notes & Quarter Notes

- Let's play this song that uses Half Notes (2 beats or counts) and Quarter Notes (1 beat or count).
- It is for the Right Hand (RH).
- Try to count aloud (1,2,3,4) for each measure. *Have fun!*

RH

Notes: **C D E F G**
Finger Numbers: **1 2 3 4 5**

Summer Day

The numbers are for the <u>beats.</u>

4/4	G F E C	D D D D	G F E C	D D C C
Beats:	1 2 3 4	1 2 3 4	1 2 3 4	1 2 3 4

	F C	G C	F E D C	D D E
	1 2 3 4	1 2 3 4	1 2 3 4	1 2 3 4

	F C	G C	F E D C	D D C
	1 2 3 4	1 2 3 4	1 2 3 4	1 2 3 4

43

In the Moonlight: A Five-Note Song with Half, Whole & Quarter Notes

- Try this song that uses Quarter Notes (1 beat), Half Notes (2 beats) and Whole Notes (4 beats).
- It is for the Right Hand (RH).
- Count aloud or in your mind (1,2,3,4) for each measure.

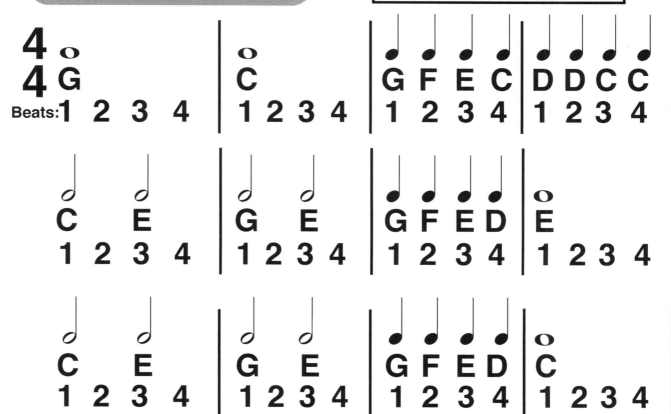

RH

Notes: **C D E F G**

Finger Numbers: **1 2 3 4 5**

In the Moonlight

The numbers are for the <u>beats.</u>

$\frac{4}{4}$ G — Beats: 1 2 3 4 | C — 1 2 3 4 | G F E C — 1 2 3 4 | D D C C — 1 2 3 4

C — 1 2 3 4 | E — 1 2 3 4 | G E — 1 2 3 4 | G F E D — 1 2 3 4 | E — 1 2 3 4

C — 1 2 3 4 | E — 1 2 3 4 | G E — 1 2 3 4 | G F E D — 1 2 3 4 | C — 1 2 3 4

44

Thanksgiving: A Five-Note Song with Half Notes & Quarter Notes

- Try this song that uses half notes (2 beats or counts) and quarter notes (1 beat or count).
- All of the songs on this page are for the Left Hand (LH).
- Try to count aloud (1,2,3,4) for each measure.

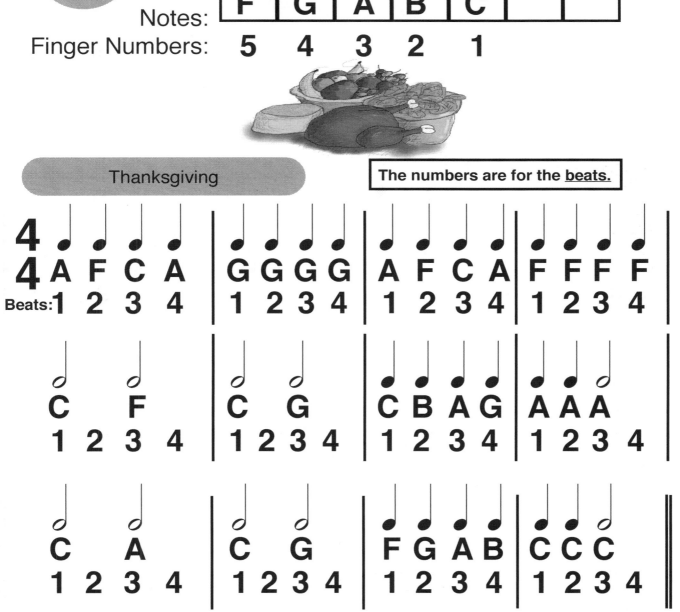

LH

Notes: F G A B C (MIDDLE)
Finger Numbers: 5 4 3 2 1

Thanksgiving

The numbers are for the **beats.**

$\frac{4}{4}$

A F C A | G G G G | A F C A | F F F F
Beats: 1 2 3 4 | 1 2 3 4 | 1 2 3 4 | 1 2 3 4

C F | C G | C B A G | A A A
1 2 3 4 | 1 2 3 4 | 1 2 3 4 | 1 2 3 4

C A | C G | F G A B | C C C
1 2 3 4 | 1 2 3 4 | 1 2 3 4 | 1 2 3 4

45

Happy Trees: A Five-Note Song with Half, Whole & Quarter Notes

- Let's play this song that uses Quarter Notes (1 beat), Half Notes (2 beats) and Whole Notes (4 beats or counts).
- It is for the Left Hand (LH).
- Try to count aloud (1,2,3,4) for each measure.

LH

Notes: F G A B C

Finger Numbers: 5 4 3 2 1

Happy Trees

| The numbers are for the <u>beats.</u> |

o
G
Beats: 1 2 3 4

o
C
1 2 3 4

G F A C
1 2 3 4

o
G
1 2 3 4

C   A
1   2   3   4

G   F
1   2   3   4

C A G F
1 2 3 4

o
G
1 2 3 4

C   A
1   2   3   4

F   G
1   2   3   4

F G A C
1 2 3 4

o
F
1 2 3 4

46

The Treble Clef

Treble Clef Notes: Middle C, D, and E

- Now, we are going to learn a little bit about the Treble Clef.
- The Treble Clef is mainly used for notes above Middle C.
- About 90% of the time, it is used for the Right Hand. (There are a few occasions in songs or pieces when it is used for the Left Hand.)
- The Treble Clef is made up of Lines and Spaces that correspond to keys on the piano. Each Line or Space is linked to <u>one</u> (and only one) key on the piano.
- We will learn more about the lines and spaces of the Treble Clef in the following lessons.

Check out video 7

Middle C

This is the TrebleClef Symbol:

Middle C is under the Treble Clef. There is a line through the middle of the note.

Note:

Finger Number: **1**

RH

D

D is under the Treble Clef, as well. It hangs under the lowest line of the Treble Clef.

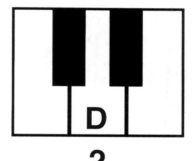

Note:

Finger Number: **2**

RH

E

E is on the first line of the Treble Clef.

Note:

Finger Number: **3**

RH

Treble Clef Exercises:
Middle C, D, and E (RH)

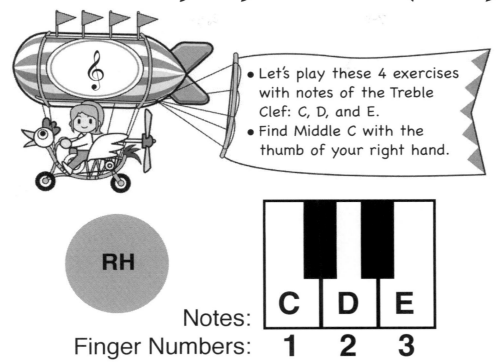

- Let's play these 4 exercises with notes of the Treble Clef: C, D, and E.
- Find Middle C with the thumb of your right hand.

RH

Notes: C D E
Finger Numbers: **1 2 3**

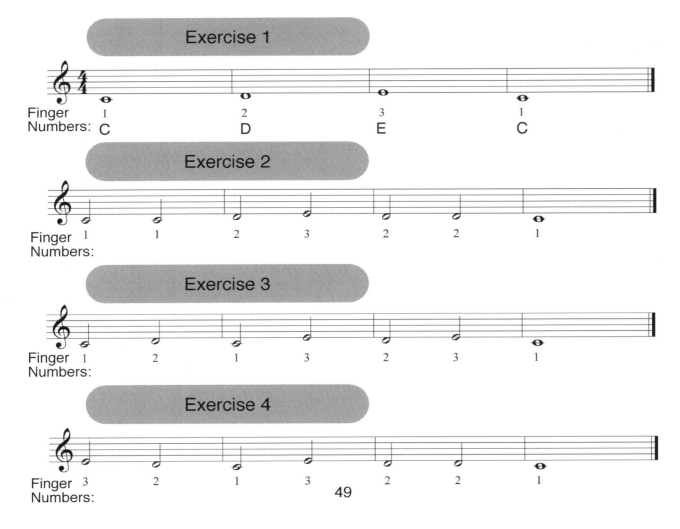

Exercise 1

Finger Numbers: 1 2 3 1
C D E C

Exercise 2

Finger Numbers: 1 1 2 3 2 2 1

Exercise 3

Finger Numbers: 1 2 1 3 2 3 1

Exercise 4

Finger Numbers: 3 2 1 3 2 2 1

Treble Clef Exercises: Middle C, D, E, & F

• Let's add the note F, which is on the 1st space of the Treble Clef.
• Remember to find Middle C with the Thumb of your right hand (RH).

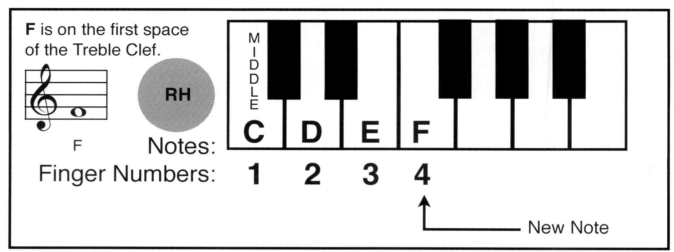

F is on the first space of the Treble Clef.

F

RH

Notes: C D E F

Finger Numbers: 1 2 3 4

New Note

Exercise 1

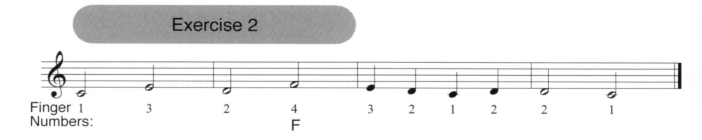

Finger Numbers: 3 2 1 2 4 4 3 3 3 2 1 2 4 4 1 1
F   F

Exercise 2

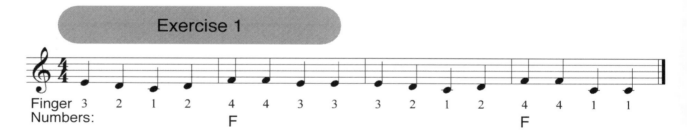

Finger Numbers: 1 3 2 4 3 2 1 2 2 1
F

Exercise 3

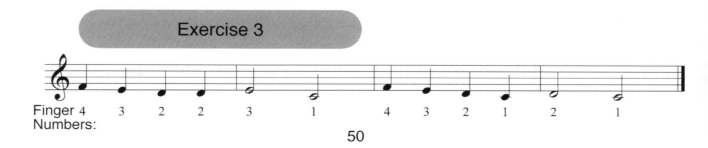

Finger Numbers: 4 3 2 2 3 1 4 3 2 1 2 1

50

The Treble Clef Lines: Overview

- Each line of the Treble Clef stands for a specific note and key on the piano.
- The lines have numbers that go from 1 to 5. Line 1 is the lowest line. Line 5 is the top line (or highest line) on the Treble Clef.
- To help you remember the note names of each line, memorize the saying below. In the saying ("Every Good Bird Does Fly"). "Every" stands for "E", "Good" stands for "G", "Bird" stands for "B", "Does" stands for "D", and "Fly" stands for "F".
- The "E" of "Every" stands for the "E" piano key 2 notes above Middle C. See the charts below to better understand these notes.

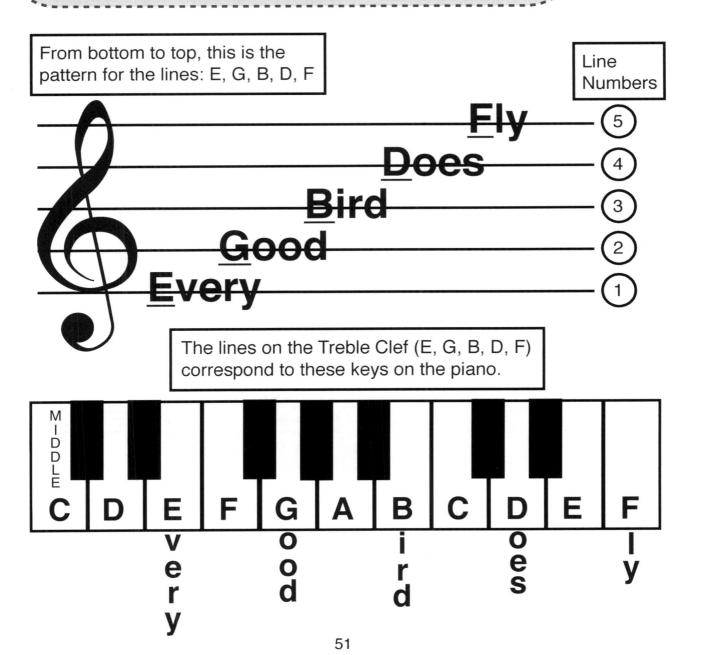

From bottom to top, this is the pattern for the lines: E, G, B, D, F

Line Numbers

Fly — 5
Does — 4
Bird — 3
Good — 2
Every — 1

The lines on the Treble Clef (E, G, B, D, F) correspond to these keys on the piano.

MIDDLE C D E F G A B C D E F

E-very
G-ood
B-ird
D-oes
F-ly

The Treble Clef Spaces: Overview

- Each space of the Treble Clef stands for a specific note and key on the piano.
- The spaces have numbers that go from 1 to 4. Space 1 is the lowest space. Space 4 is the top space (or highest space) on the Treble Clef.
- To help you learn the note names of each space, remember that the spaces of the Treble Clef form the word "Face" spelled upside down (from bottom space to top.)
- The "F" of "Face" stands for the "F" piano key 4 notes above Middle C.
- See the charts below to better understand the other notes.

From bottom to top, this is the pattern for the Spaces: F, A, C, E

Space Numbers

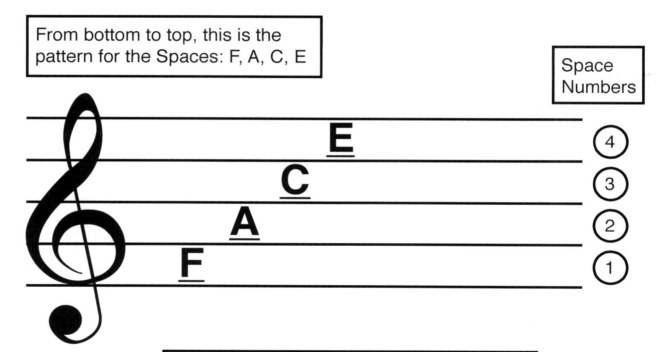

The spaces on the Treble Clef (F, A, C, E) correspond to these keys on the piano.

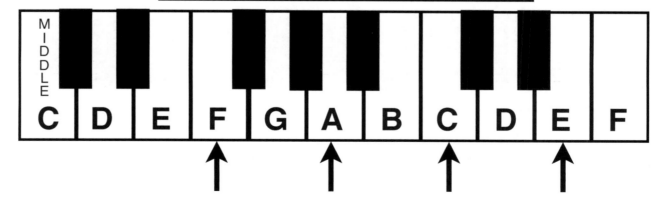

Kum-Bah-Yah:
New Notes: G and A

- Let's add 2 new notes G and A, which are on the 2nd line and space of the Treble Clef.
- Remember to find Middle C with the Thumb of your right hand (RH).

G is on the 2nd line of the Treble Clef.

A is on the 2nd space of the Treble Clef.

Move your pinky from G to A, in order to play

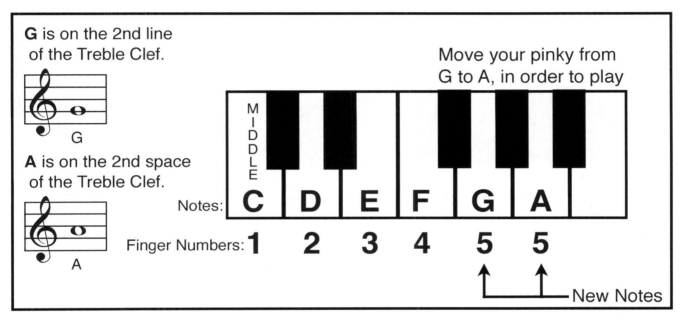

Notes:	C	D	E	F	G	A
Finger Numbers:	1	2	3	4	5	5

New Notes

Kum-Bah-Yah

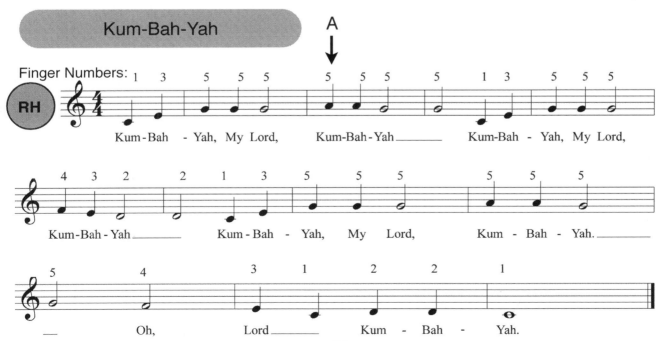

Finger Numbers: 1 3 5 5 5 5 5 5 5 1 3 5 5 5

RH

Kum-Bah - Yah, My Lord,   Kum-Bah-Yah_____   Kum-Bah - Yah, My Lord,

4 3 2 2 1 3 5 5 5 5 5 5

Kum-Bah - Yah_____   Kum - Bah - Yah, My Lord,   Kum - Bah - Yah.

5 4 3 1 2 2 1

___   Oh,   Lord_____   Kum - Bah - Yah.

53

The Bass Clef

The Bass Clef: Middle C, B & A

- The Bass Clef mainly is used for notes below Middle C.
- About 90% of the time, it is used for the Left Hand.
  (There are a few occasions in songs when it is used for the Right Hand.)
- The word "Bass" is pronounced like the word "Base" (as in "Baseball").
- The Bass Clef is made up of Lines and Spaces that correspond to keys on the piano. Each Line or Space is linked to <u>one</u> (and only one) key on the piano.
- We will learn more about the lines and spaces of the Bass Clef in the following lessons.

Middle C

This is the Bass Clef Symbol: 𝄢

Middle C is above the Bass Clef. There is a line through the middle of the note.

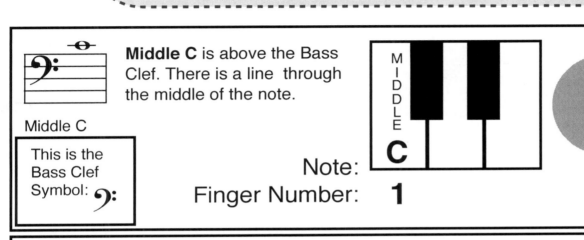

Note: **C**

Finger Number: **1**

LH

B

B is on the Bass Clef. It sits on top of the highest line of the Bass Clef.

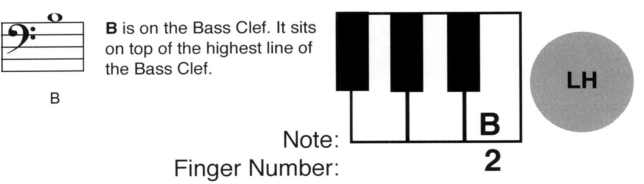

Note: **B**

Finger Number: **2**

LH

A

A is on the fifth line of the Bass Clef.

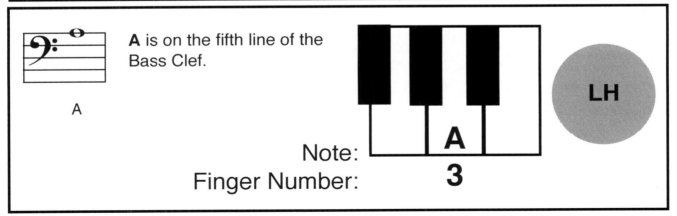

Note: **A**

Finger Number: **3**

LH

55

The Bass Clef: A, B & Middle C

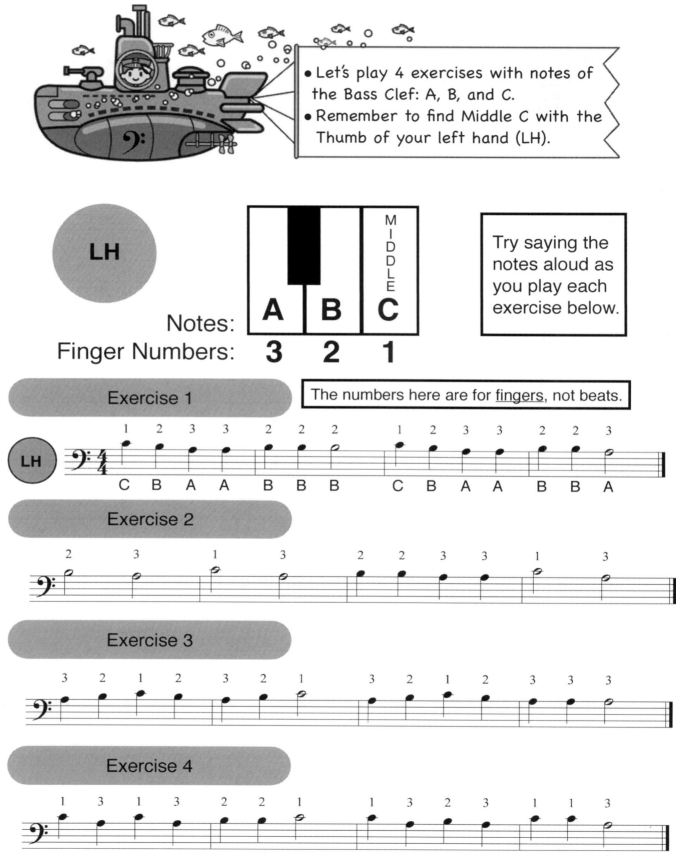

- Let's play 4 exercises with notes of the Bass Clef: A, B, and C.
- Remember to find Middle C with the Thumb of your left hand (LH).

LH

Notes: A B C (MIDDLE C)
Finger Numbers: 3 2 1

Try saying the notes aloud as you play each exercise below.

Exercise 1

The numbers here are for <u>fingers</u>, not beats.

LH — 9: 4/4
1 2 3 3 2 2 2 | 1 2 3 3 2 2 3
C B A A B B B | C B A A B B A

Exercise 2

2 3 1 3 2 2 3 3 1 3

Exercise 3

3 2 1 2 3 2 1 3 2 1 2 3 3 3

Exercise 4

1 3 1 3 2 2 1 1 3 2 3 1 1 3

The Bass Clef Notes:
G, A, B & Middle C

- Let's add the note G, which is on the 4th space of the Bass Clef.
- Remember to find Middle C with the Thumb of your right hand (LH).

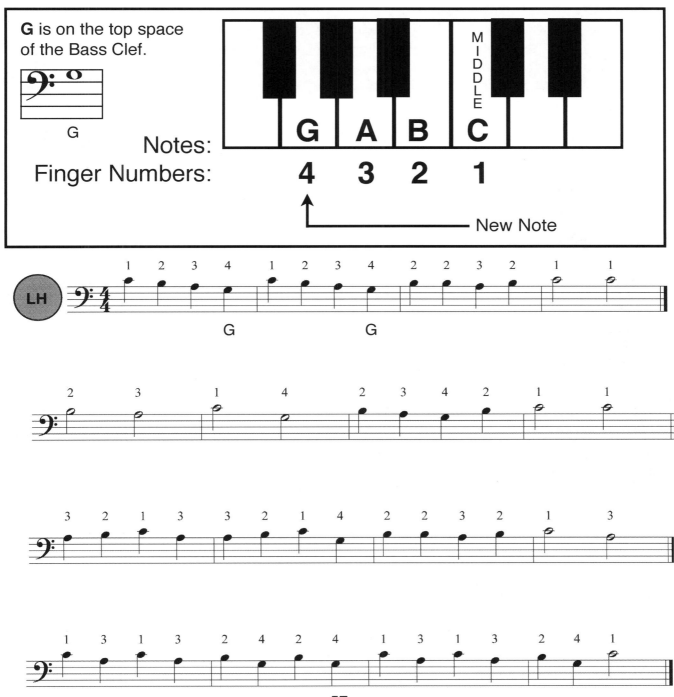

The Bass Clef Lines: Overview

- Each line of the Bass Clef stands for a specific note and key on the piano.
- The lines have numbers that go from 1 to 5. Line 1 is the lowest line. Line 5 is the top line (or highest line) on the Bass Clef.
- To help you remember the note names of each line, memorize the saying below. In the saying ("Good Baked Desserts For All"). "Good" stands for "G", "Baked" stands for "B", "Desserts" stands for "D", "For" stands for "F", and "All" stands for "A".
- The "A" of "All" stands for the "A" piano key 2 notes below Middle C. See the charts below to better understand these notes.

Check out video 8

From bottom to top, this is the pattern for the lines: G, B, D, F, A

Line Numbers

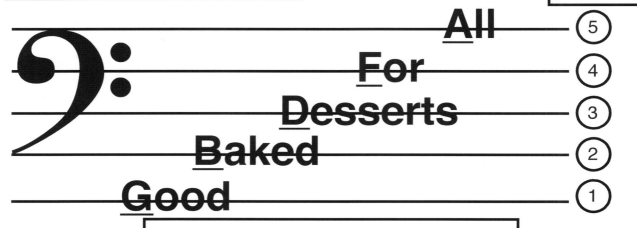

The lines on the Bass Clef (G, B, D, F, A) correspond to these keys on the piano.

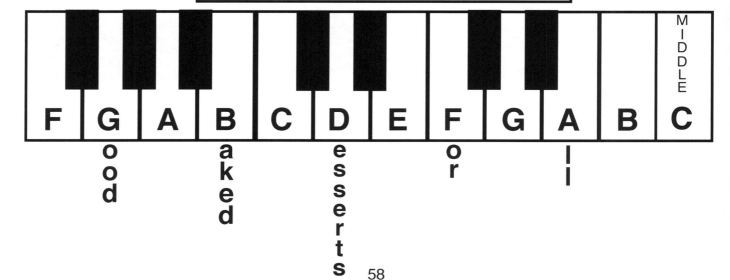

58

The Bass Clef Spaces: Overview

- Each space of the Bass Clef stands for a specific note and key on the piano.
- The spaces have numbers that go from 1 to 4. Space 1 is the lowest space. Space 4 is the top space (or highest space) on the Bass Clef.
- To help you learn the note names of each space, remember that the spaces of the Bass Clef form the phrase "All cows eat grass".
- The word "All" stands for the key and note "A"; the word "Cows" stands for "C".
- See the charts below to better understand the other notes.

Space Numbers

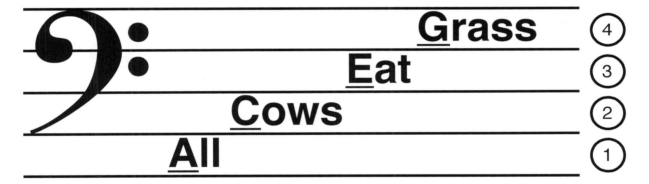

The spaces on the Bass Clef (A, C, E, G) correspond to these keys on the piano.

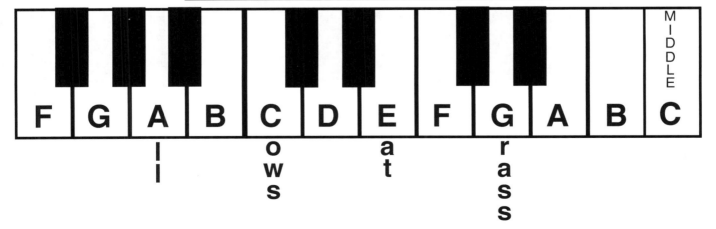

59

Bass Clef Exercises:
F, G, A, B, & Middle C

- Let's add the note F, which is on the 4th line of the Bass Clef.
- Remember to find Middle C with the Thumb of your left hand (LH).

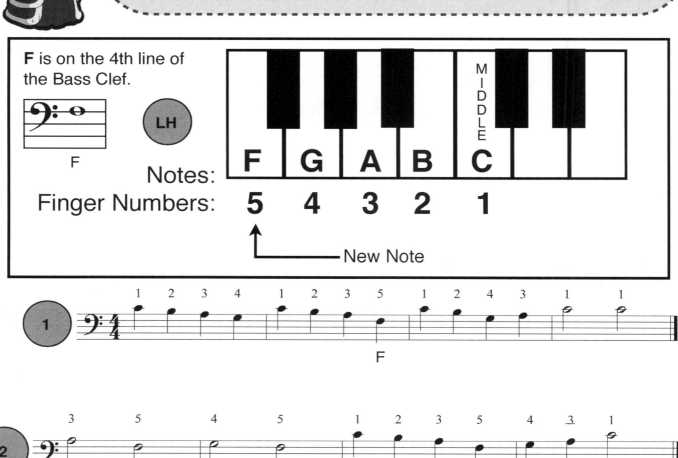

F is on the 4th line of the Bass Clef.

F

LH

Notes: F   G   A   B   C

Finger Numbers: 5   4   3   2   1

↑ — New Note

1 1 2 3 4 1 2 3 5 1 2 4 3 1 1

F

2 3 5 4 5 1 2 3 5 4 3 1

3 3 2 1 3 4 3 2 4 5 4 3 5 4 1

4 1 3 1 3 2 4 2 4 3 5 3 5 4 2 1

Bass Clef Exercises:
F, G, A, B, & Middle C

• Let's add the note F, which is on the 4th line of the Bass Clef.
• Remember to find Middle C with the Thumb of your left hand (LH).

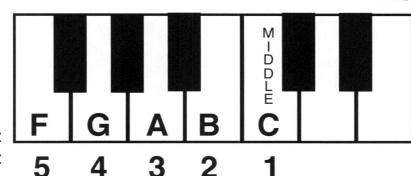

Notes: F G A B C
Finger Numbers: 5 4 3 2 1

Exercise 1

Exercise 2

Exercise 3

Exercise 4

The Grand Staff

Overview: The Grand Staff

- The Grand Staff is formed by combining the Treble and Bass Clefs.
- All of the rules that we have learned so far about both clefs are still true for the Grand Staff. Using the Grand Staff makes it easier to read music written for both hands.
- Study the chart below to understand how the Staff works.

Check out video 9

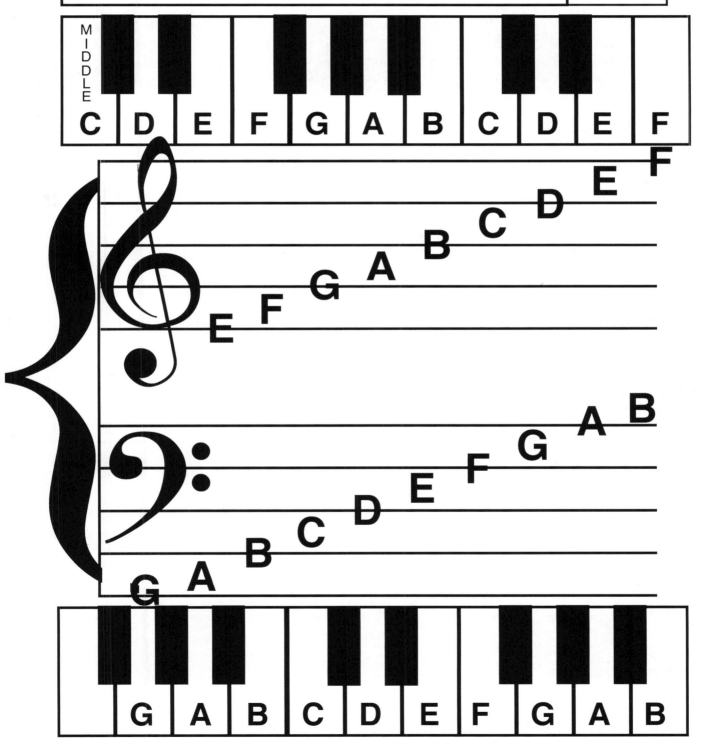

Naming the Notes on the Grand Staff

For this lesson, let's try naming the notes on the grand staff below. Remember to use your note-name sayings from earlier in the book. You may also refer back to the grand staff on the previous page. Try naming the notes for one measure, then go back and repeat naming the notes for that measure three times. Once you feel confident about the note names, go on to the next measure. After you have finished naming the notes on the entire page, go back to the beginning of the lesson and slowly play each note on the piano. You might also say the note aloud as you play it. This will begin to reinforce your understanding of the notes on the page and the keys on the piano keyboard.

Simple Gifts

For *Simple Gifts,* your right-hand thumb will be on Middle C. Your left-hand thumb should be placed on the B, directly to the left of Middle C. (See chart below.)

To make the music easier to read, the note names are written inside of the notes and the finger numbers are indicated above the notes.

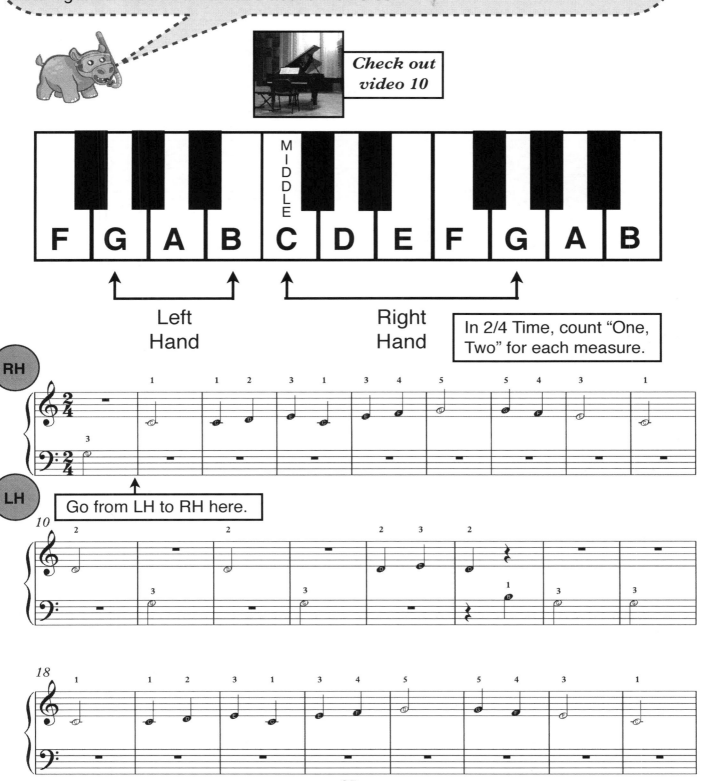

Check out video 10

Left Hand

Right Hand

In 2/4 Time, count "One, Two" for each measure.

Go from LH to RH here.

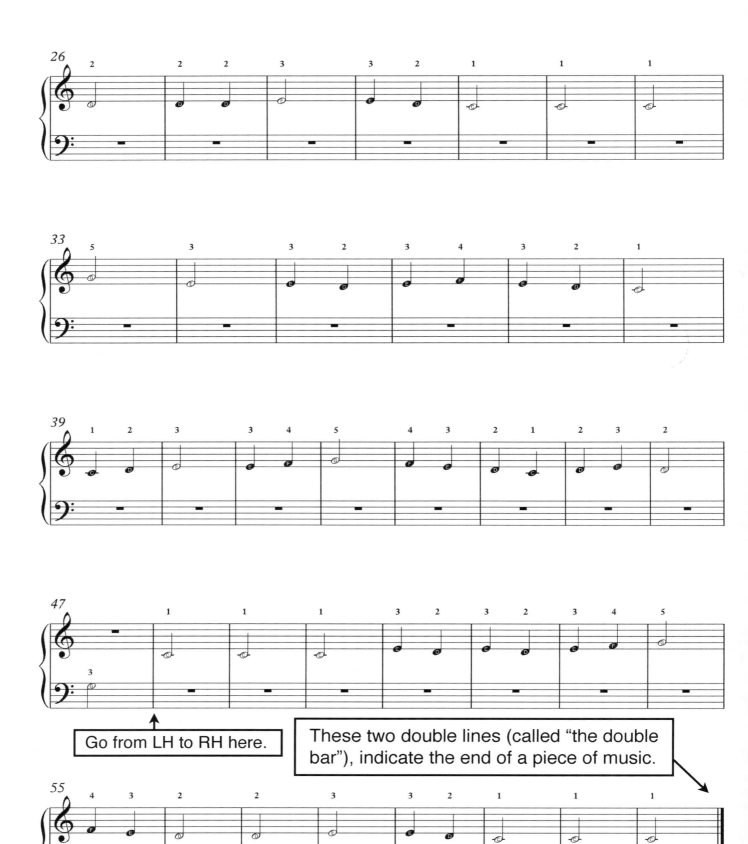

Go from LH to RH here.

These two double lines (called "the double bar"), indicate the end of a piece of music.

Amazing Grace

- *Amazing Grace* is in 3/4 Time. Remember to count "One, Two, Three" for each measure.
- The melody goes between the left and right hands many times.
- Please hold the dotted half note for three beats (or counts). See the example below:

$\bf{\large d}$. = 3 Beats

Check out video 11

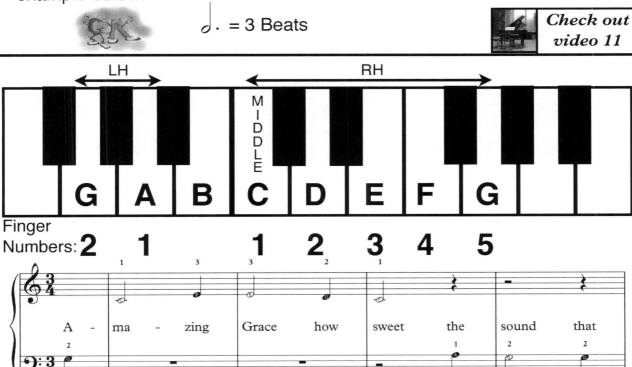

Jingle Bells

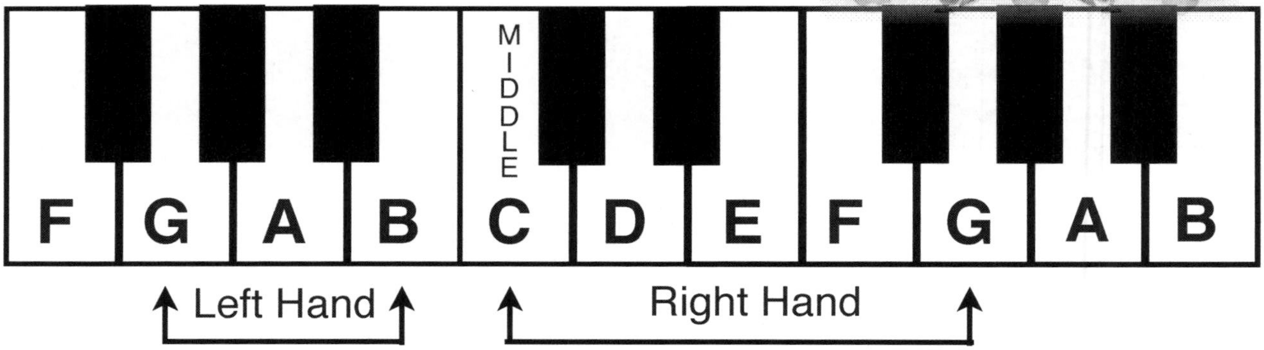

F G A B C D E F G A B

↑ Left Hand ↑   ↑ Right Hand ↑

The letter names are indicated
inside the notes for this song.

This is a quarter rest
(silence) for one beat.

Dash - ing through the   snow   in   one   horse   o - pen

Go from LH to RH here.

Go from LH to RH here.

This is a half rest
(silence) for two beats.

sleighs;   o're   the   fields   we   go,

This is a whole note;
hold for four beats.

laugh - ing   all   the   way!   The

bells   on   bob - tails   ring,   They're

68

Michael, Row the Boat Ashore

• *Michael, Row the Boat Ashore* is in 4/4 Time. Remember to count "One, Two, Three, Four" for each measure.
• Both right-hand and left-hand thumbs share Middle C.
• This song also goes back and forth between the hands. Take a glance at the music and look for patterns of hand switching before you start playing the music.
• Lastly, we have left out the letter names from inside the notes for this song. Refer back to the Grand Staff, if you have questions.

Surfing the Waves

In May

- Slurs (or Phrase Markers) are curved lines that go over or under two or more different notes in piano music.
- They indicate two things: to play a passage or phrase with a smooth sound ("legato", which means smooth or connected notes played) and slurs (or phrase markers) also indicate where a musical phrase (the musical equivalent to a sentence) starts and ends.
- For *In May*, both the right-hand and left-hand thumbs will share Middle C. Before playing the piece, take a glance at the page and make a note of the places where the melody goes from the right hand to the left hand. Try to anticipate these shifts while you play the piece.

A Slur (or Phrase Marker) looks like this:

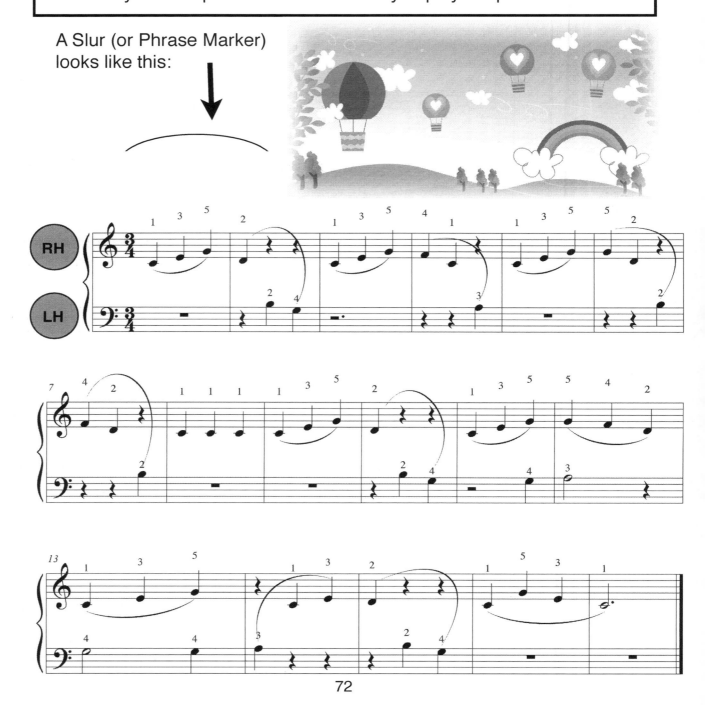

Rocket Ship

Music Theory:

Check out video 12

What are Sharps & Flats?

- On the piano, there are two types of keys: Black Keys and White Keys.
- The White Keys stand for natural notes, for example, C, D, E, F, G, A and B.
- The Black Keys (also called "accidentals") stand for Sharp or Flat Notes.
- Sharp Notes use this symbol: #
- Flat Notes use this symbol: ♭
- Here are some examples of Sharp Notes: F#, G#, A#, C#, D#
- Here are some examples of Flat Notes: Gb, Ab, Bb, Db, Eb

- On the piano keyboard, Sharp Keys are located directly to the right of their corresponding Natural Key (White Key). For example, F Sharp (F#) is the next key to the right from F (also called "F Natural"). C Sharp (C#) is the black key directly to the right of C (also called "C Natural").
- This pattern, of going to the next key directly to the right, holds true for all of the sharp notes going up and down the piano keyboard.
- Using the chart below, try locating the following sharp keys on the piano: C#, F#, D#, A#, G#.

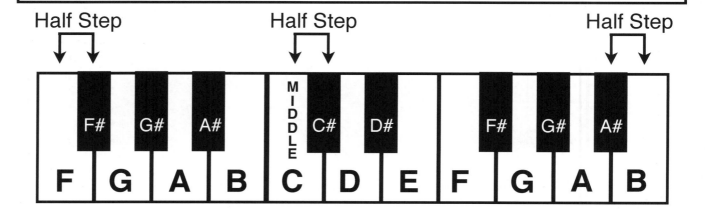

- The distance from a White Key to a Black Key, for example, F to F#, C to C#, or A# to B, is called a **Half Step** or Minor Second. **Remember this.** It is a bit of important information; we will be referring to it later in this book.

Music Theory
More on Flats and Sharps

- On the piano keyboard, Flat Keys are located directly to the left of their corresponding Natural Key (White Key). For example, G Flat (Gb) is the next black key to the left from G (also called "G Natural"). E Flat (Eb) is the black key directly to the left of E (also called "E Natural").
- This pattern, of going to the next key directly to the left, holds true for all of the flat notes going up and down the piano keyboard.
- Using the chart below, try locating the following flat keys on the piano: Ab, Db, Gb, Eb, Bb. **Remember: This pattern is the same for the entire keyboard.**

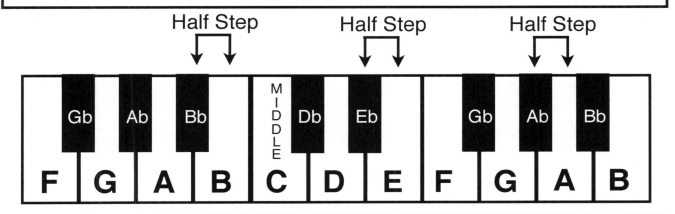

- The distance (up or down) from a White Key to a Black Key, for example, from B to Bb, Eb to E, or A to Ab, is called a Half Step or Minor Second. See Above.

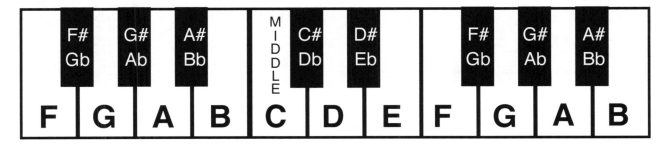

- You might have noticed in the last two lessons that there are 2 names for each Black Key: A Sharp Name and a Flat Name. This is true for the entire piano.
- Depending on the musical context (which we will learn more about throughout this book), a black key may be called by either its sharp or flat name. For example, A Flat and G Sharp are the same key on the piano; C Sharp and D Flat are the same key; and F Sharp and G Flat are the same key. See Above.

Scarborough Fair

- *Scarborough Fair* is in 3/4 Time.
  Count: One, Two, Three
- For the F#, play the black key directly
  to the right of F on the piano.

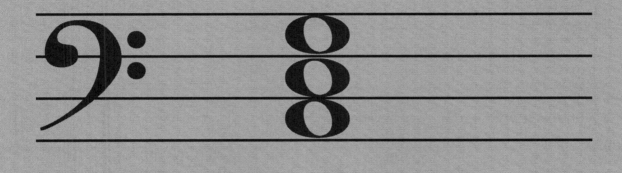

Easy Chords

Easy Chords Overview:
C Major, F Major & G7

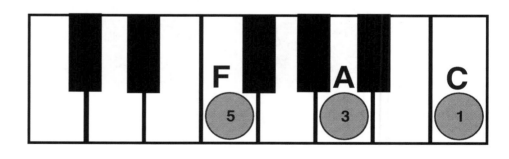

- Chords are 3 or more notes played at the same time.
- In order to play chords well, keep your fingers curved for the notes that you play and lift your fingers that are not being used for the chord.
- Take a look at video lesson 16 to see and hear how these techniques work.
- For these chords, use the Left Hand (LH).
- We are going to look at 3 chords in this lesson.

Check out video 13

C Major

C Major

The numbers are for the fingers.

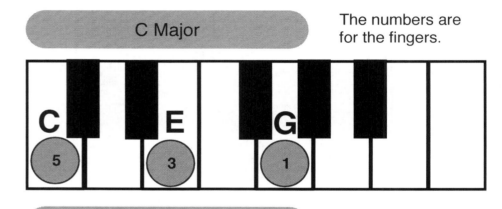

F Major

F Major

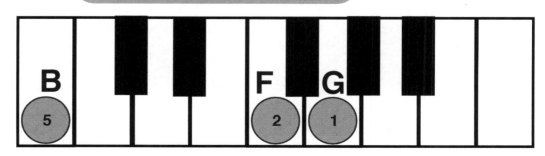

G7

G7

More Easy Chords
A Minor, D Minor & G

- Let's look at 3 more chords for the Left Hand: A Minor, D Minor, & G Major.
- Make sure to keep your fingers curved and lift the fingers that do not play.
- Listen to the difference in sound between the major and minor chords.

The numbers are for the fingers.

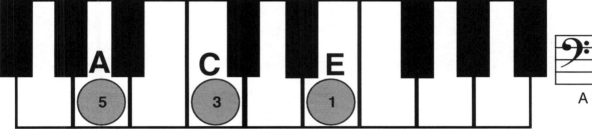

A Minor

A Minor

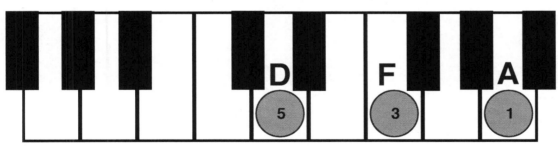

D Minor

D Minor

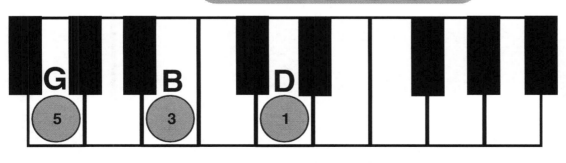

G Major

G Major

Chord Overview & Exercise

In this lesson, we are going to practice playing some of the chords from the previous two lessons. With each of these exercises, take your time to master the transition from one chord to the next. Building up this kind of left-hand coordination will greatly help you, once we start learning the songs with left-hand chords from the next section of the book. If you have a metronome, you might set it to quarter note equals 60 (in other words sixty beats per minute) for this exercise. As a side note, there are many free metronome apps available online. If you have a smart phone, tablet, computer, or similar electronic device, you might take a moment to find a free metronome app for it online; you can use a metronome to help you learn the pieces later in the book.

When you move from one chord to the next, try to form the new chord with your fingers, before playing the keys. This technique will improve your muscle memory for the chords. Along these lines, try to avoid sliding your fingers along the keyboard to find the notes of the chords. This will not only hamper the development of your muscle memory for playing chords, but it will also make it more likely that you will play a few wrong notes.

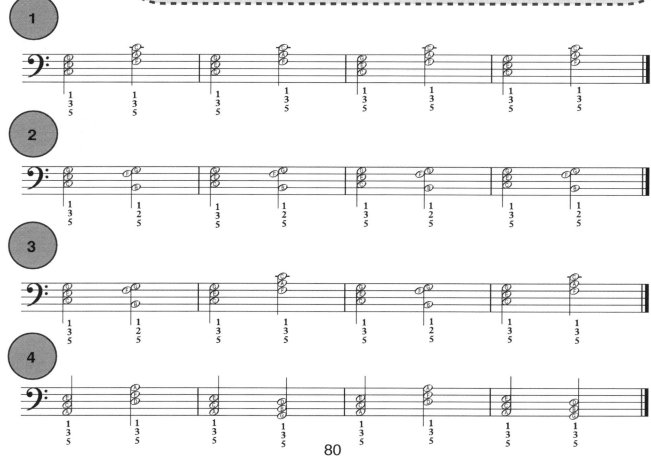

Panda Dance:
C Major & G7 Chords

* This song is in 4/4 Time. There are 4 beats per measure.
* The song has C Major and G7 chords. **Have Fun!**

C
Chord

G7
Chord

Red River Valley

Aura Lee

82

Ode to Joy, Chord Version

- This version of Ode to Joy uses the C Major and G7 Chords.
- Remember to count the beats as you play.
- The piece is in 4/4 Time: 4 Beats per measure.

Check out video 14

Ode to Joy

RH
LH

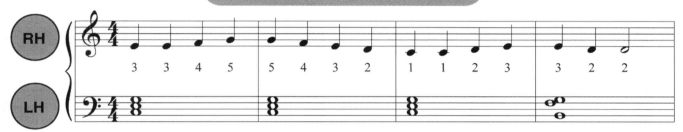

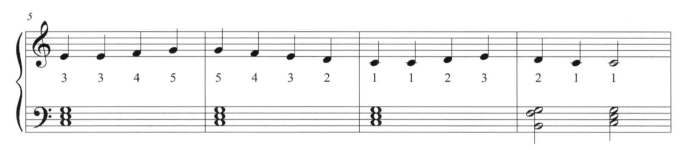

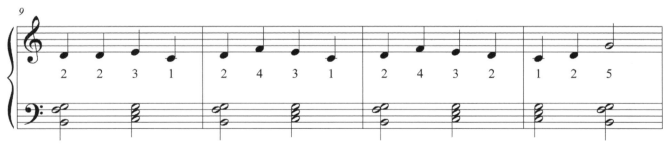

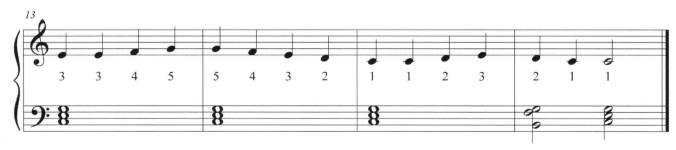

Happy Dog

- Happy Dog is in 4/4 Time (4 Beats per Measure).
- The melody has quarter notes and half notes.
- The chords are in the left hand.
- The melody is in the right hand.
- Play the chords on the first beat of each measure.

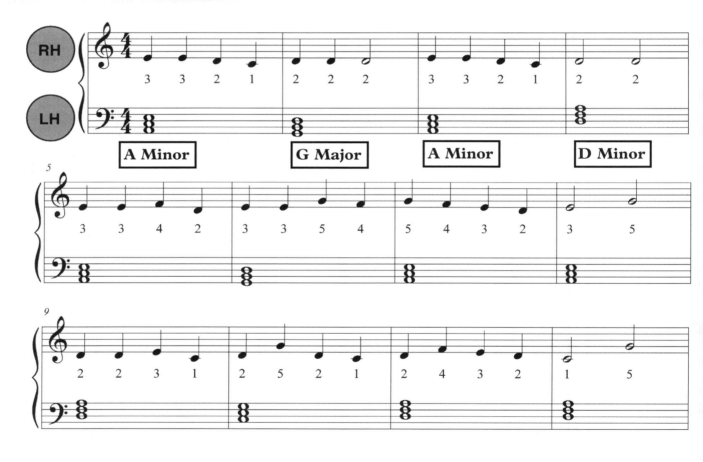

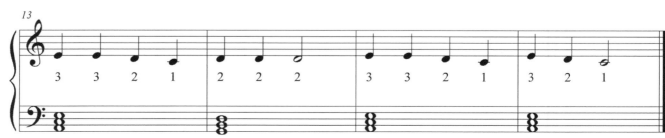

House of the Rising Sun

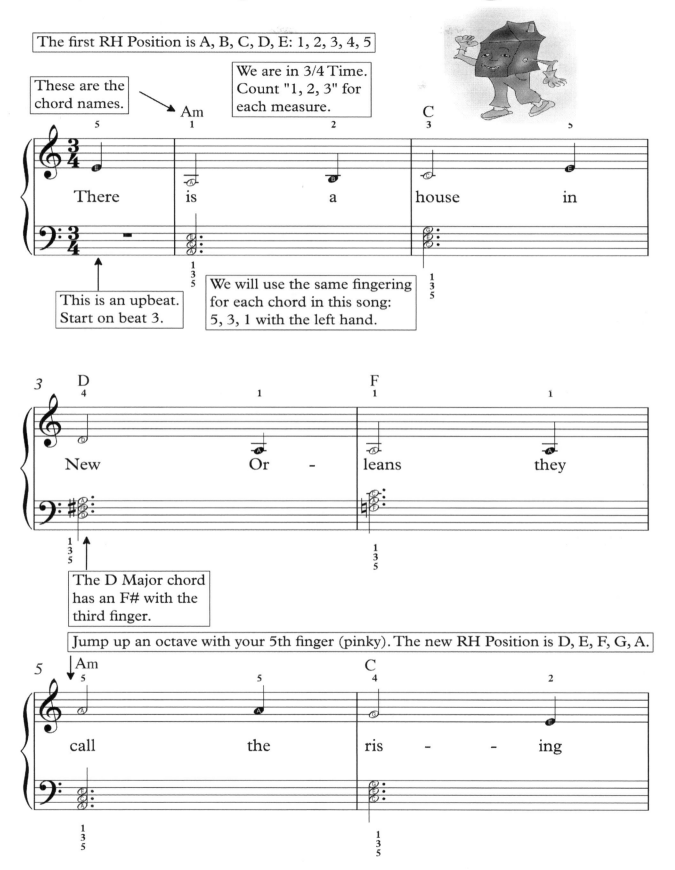

The first RH Position is A, B, C, D, E: 1, 2, 3, 4, 5

These are the chord names.

We are in 3/4 Time. Count "1, 2, 3" for each measure.

This is an upbeat. Start on beat 3.

We will use the same fingering for each chord in this song: 5, 3, 1 with the left hand.

There is a house in

New Or - leans they

The D Major chord has an F# with the third finger.

Jump up an octave with your 5th finger (pinky). The new RH Position is D, E, F, G, A.

call the ris - - ing

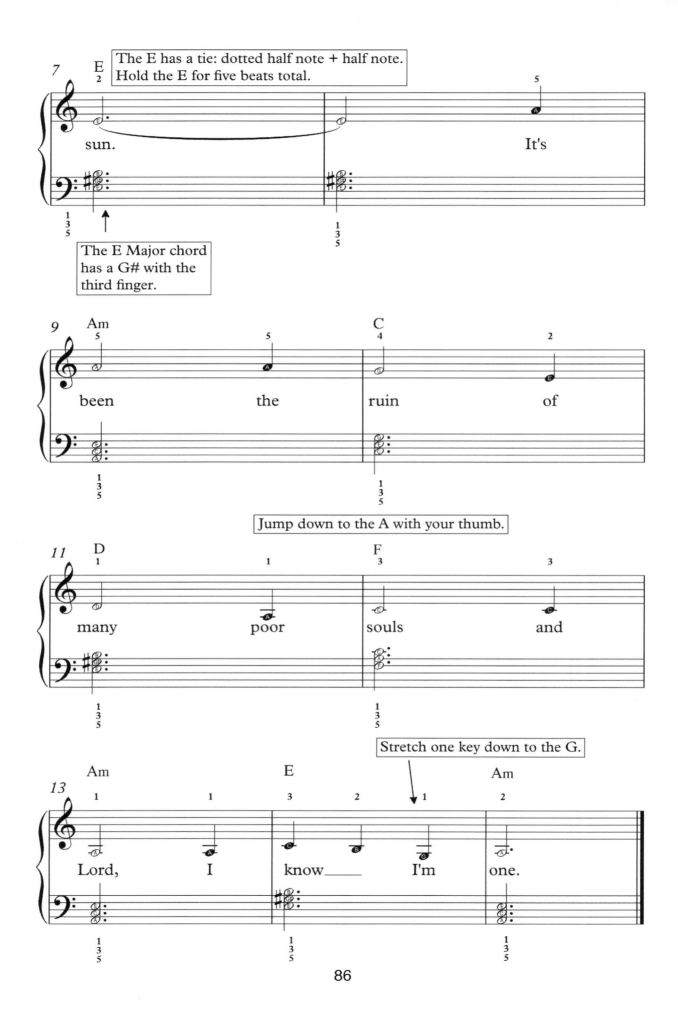

The E has a tie: dotted half note + half note.
Hold the E for five beats total.

sun. It's

The E Major chord
has a G# with the
third finger.

been the ruin of

Jump down to the A with your thumb.

many poor souls and

Stretch one key down to the G.

Lord, I know____ I'm one.

86

We have four new chords for *Happy Birthday:*

G in First Inversion:
the note B is in the bass.
Use fingers 5, 3, 1.

F in First Inversion:
the note A is in the bass.
Use fingers 5, 3, 1.

F in Second Inversion:
the note C is in the bass.
Use fingers 5, 2, 1

Bb
Major
Use fingers 5, 3, 1

Happy Birthday

These letters are
the chord names.

The note names are
inside the notes.

Hap — py   birth — — day

to   you.   The curved line is a tie:
Hold the E for 6 beats.

Hap — py   birth — — day

87

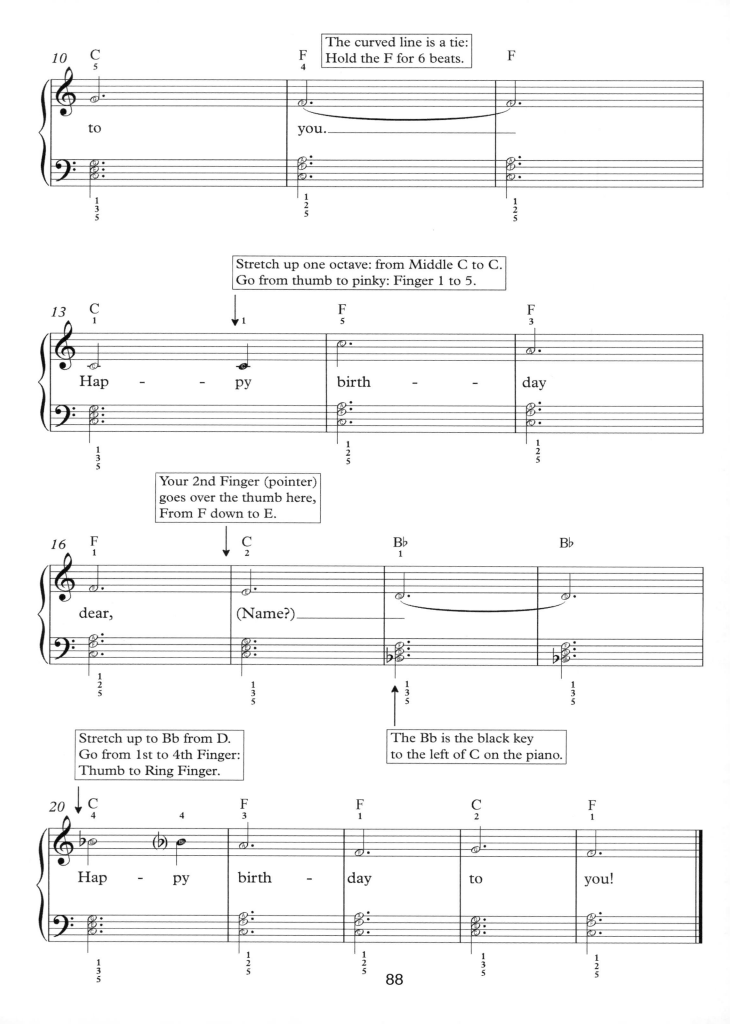

Music Theory: Overview of Dynamics

As we continue, let's look at a few music concepts that come up in some songs and pieces of music.

Dynamics is a term that we use for the loudness and softness of the notes in music. In pieces and songs you will see dynamic indications represented as letters (F, P, MP, or MF, for example). These letters are abbreviations for Italian words.

 stands for the term "piano", which means soft
(like a whisper, but not the quietest whisper).

 stands for the term "mezzo-piano", which means medium soft
(like a quiet conversation).

 stands for the term "mezzo-forte", which means medium loud
(like a normal conversation).

 stands for the term "forte", which means loud (like a shout).

Dynamics are a relative concept in music. In other words, you might consider that each piece has a slightly different range from soft to loud. Forte ("loud") in the context of a Beethoven piece may be a little different than forte in a Mozart piece. So, let's think of dynamics as a general concept that vary slightly from piece to piece. Part of what makes music so exciting and inspiring is finding the nuance and detail in the poetics of each piece.

. . . .

In piano sheet music (sometimes called the "score"), we are given indications on how to make the music gradually louder or softer. In a lighthearted way, you might think of this as the piano version of turning up or turning down the volume on a car stereo, TV, or an audio device. In piano music we use two symbols:

Crescendo means to get gradually louder

Diminuendo means to get gradually quieter

The Happy Cat

The note names have been added to some of the left-hand chords to help you a little bit with the song.

Use fingers 1, 3, and 5
for all of the LH chords.

The Sad Dog

The note names have been added to some of the left-hand chords to help you a little bit with the song.

Use fingers 1, 3, and 5 for all of the LH chords.

Simple Gifts Overview & Lesson

Let's look again at *Simple Gifts.* This is the wonderful Americana theme that inspired Aaron Copland in his famous piece, *Appalachian Spring.* The theme has a dancelike character, which is energized by the use of eighth notes in the melody. Eighth notes are equal to half of a quarter note and are counted as half of a beat.

They look like this:

In a measure of 4/4 time, eight eighth notes would be counted like this: 1 &, 2 &, 3 &, 4 &. The "&" stands for the word "and". The "&" or "and" is the halfway point of a beat. See the example below:

Musicians often refer to the halfway point of a beat as the "and". For example, a musician might say, "play it on the *and* of *two*". This would mean: play it at the halfway point of beats two and three.

When you divide a beat into sections, it is called "subdividing". Let's practice counting and playing groups of eighth notes and quarter notes. Remember to subdivide the eighth notes: for example, 1 &, 2 &, 3 &, 4 &.

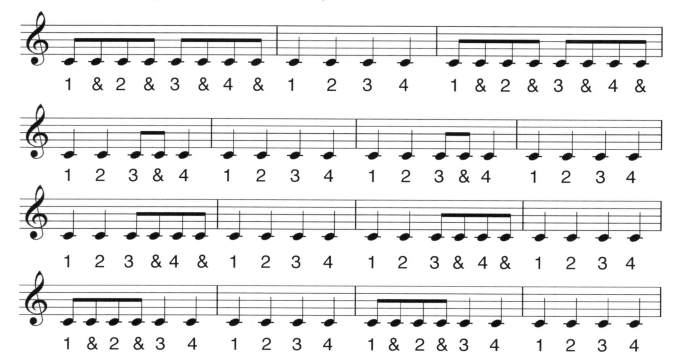

In exercise one, we discover that the melody is exchanged between the left and right hands. The melody starts in the left hand and then moves to the right hand. Also, the first note is an upbeat or pickup note. This is a device that helps emphasize part of a musical phrase. The first note (G) leans into the second note (middle C). The G will be on the fourth beat of the measure. So, count: 1, 2, 3, 4. On beat four, play the G. Then go into the next measure, the first full measure, and play middle C on the downbeat (beat one).

**Exercise
#1**

In piano music, phrases (the musical equivalent of sentences in language) are indicated by the use of slurs (or phrase markers). Slurs are curved lines that go over or under two or more different notes. When you finish a phrase in music, you should lift your hand or fingers a little bit to separate it from the next phrase. Slurs also indicate to play in a smooth (*legato*) manner on the piano. You can see some slurs in the melody for *Simple Gifts.*

**Exercise
#2**

Let's now practice the melody in the left hand, as exercise two. Start this exercise slowly and then gradually build up the speed. Make sure that you pay special attention to the finger numbers; there are a few little shifts.

Simple Gifts

Remember to subdivide for the eighth notes.

Practice the left-hand chords alone, until they are comfortable, before playing with both hands .

The note names are listed inside each note.

The dynamic marks indicate how loud or soft to play the piece. They also indicate whether the music should get gradually louder or softer.

Practice the piece slowly, mastering one system (a line of music) at time, before moving on to the next system. This way, you will learn the music faster, assembling and mastering one section of music, before moving on to the next.

The melody moves between hands here.

Practice the right-hand chords alone, until they are comfortable, before playing with both hands.

Pay attention to the finger numbers in the left hand.

Lesson on Brahms' Lullaby

Let's look at this famous lullaby by Johannes Brahms. In exercise one, we are going to focus on the left hand. This left-hand chord style of alternating a bass note with a small chord is a very common technique in piano playing. Some people refer to it as the "um, pa, pa" style, since it simulates the sound of an orchestra or band playing the accompaniment (or background music) for a melody. When playing this "um, pa, pa" style, lean your hand and wrist down slightly and to the left a little bit to emphasize the first note of the measure; in measure one, this would be low note C. Then, slightly lift your hand back to its regular position for the second two beats; for the first measures, this would be the chords with the notes E and G. Follow this same motion for the entire piece. Count 1, 2, 3 for each measure.

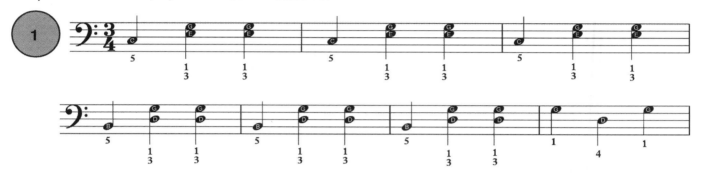

In exercise two, let's look at the beginning melody of the piece. The music is in 3/4 time signature. This means that there will be three beats in a measure and that the quarter note will get the beat. Also, the first measure is an upbeat. An upbeat is a note or set of notes that push into the downbeat (the first beat of the next measure). You might think of the phrase "the end", where the word "the" is accented to emphasize the word "end". Try saying it emphasizing the word "the": **The** end. A similar effect takes place for the two E notes that begin the melody. They are slightly accented to "push" into the G, which is the third note of the melody. Count: 1, 2, 3. On the count of three, play the upbeat E. This upbeat figure occurs several times in the lullaby.

For exercise three, let's put both hands together. Try this slowly and then gradually build up the speed to a moderate tempo. Remember to count to three (1,2, 3) for each measure. Also, remember the upbeat figure at the beginning.

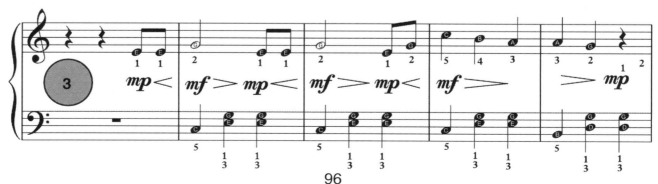

96

Lullaby

The note names are added here to make the song a bit easier.

Check out video 15

Johannes Brahms

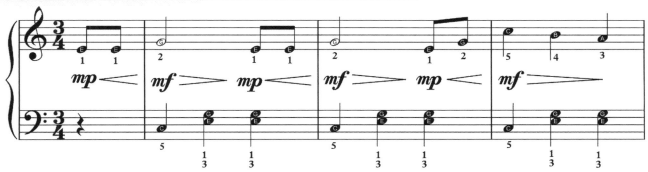

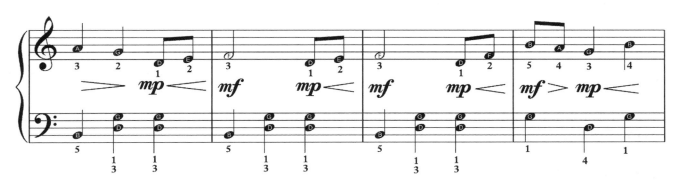

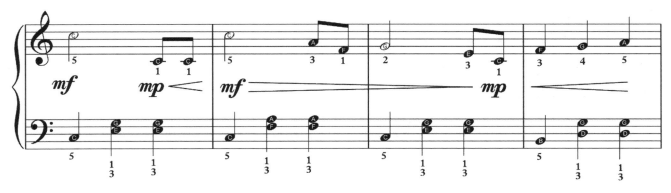

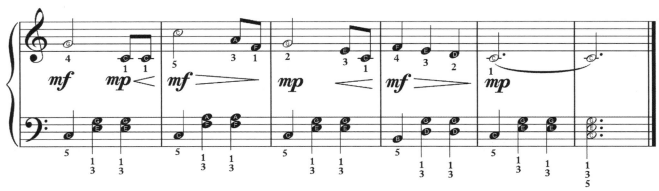

Shenandoah & Hineh Ma Tov in Um-Pah Chord Style

Shenandoah

Hineh Ma Tov

This lyrical piece is in a minor key: A Minor. Listen for the difference in sound quality.

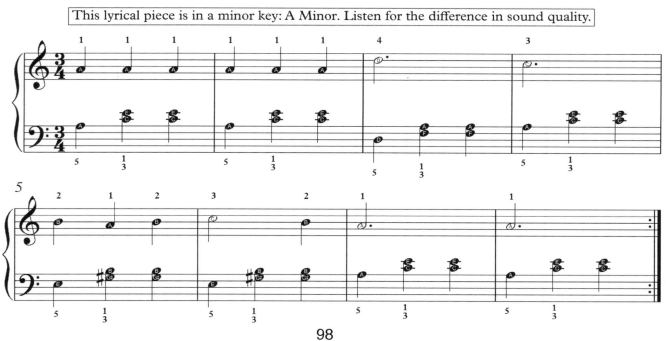

Home
On the Range

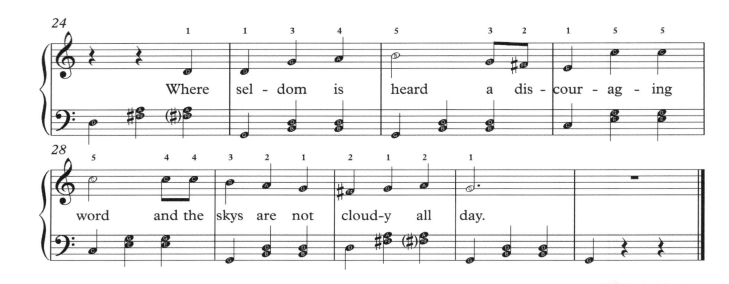

This Little Light of Mine

Congratulations!
You have completed the Book!

Great work in completing this book and video course on the basics of piano. You now have an understanding of the fundamentals of piano playing: basic piano technique, beginner-level note reading and chord playing, a repertoire of songs and pieces to perform for family and friends, and some understanding of music fundamentals--such as time signatures, beats, and the grand staff.

To continue to the next level, I would suggest two book and video courses:

1. *Beginner Classical Piano Music*
2. *Piano Scales, Chords & Arpeggio Lessons with Basic Music Theory*

Keep up the good work and continue to practice and play the piano!

Damon Ferrante

If you enjoyed this book, please recommend the paperback edition to your local library.

Damon Ferrante is a composer, guitarist, and professor of piano studies. He has taught on the music faculties of Seton Hall University and Montclair State University. For over 20 years, Damon has taught guitar, piano, composition, and music theory. Damon has had performances at Carnegie Hall, Symphony Space, and throughout the US and Europe. His main teachers have been David Rakowski at Columbia University, Stanley Wolfe at Juilliard, and Bruno Amato at the Peabody Conservatory of Johns Hopkins University. Damon has written two operas, a guitar concerto, song cycles, orchestral music, and numerous solo and chamber music works. He has over 30 music books and scores in print. For more information on his books, concerts, and music, please visit steeplechasearts.com.

CERTIFICATE
of ACCOMPLISHMENT

This certifies that

_____
(sign your name)

Has successfully completed the training program requirement for

Piano Book for Kids 5 & Up

and is ready to begin

BEGINNER CLASSICAL PIANO MUSIC

_____   _____
DATE   TEACHER

GREAT JOB!

Two More Best-Selling Piano Books by Damon Ferrante!

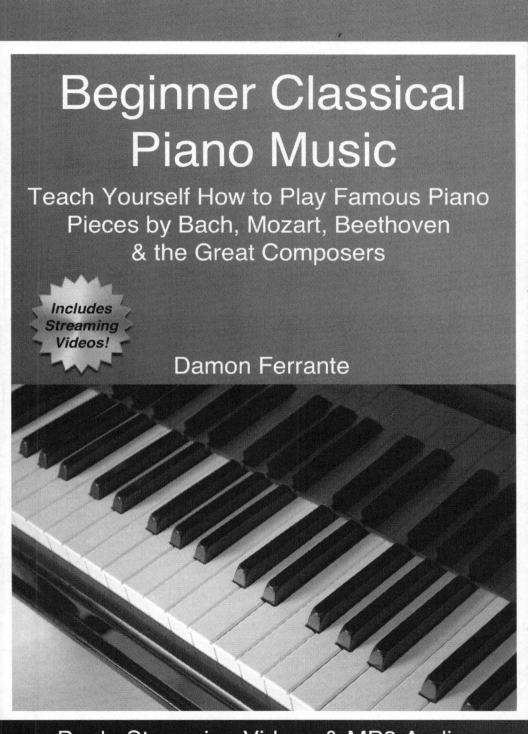

Beginner Classical Piano Music

Teach Yourself How to Play Famous Piano Pieces by Bach, Mozart, Beethoven & the Great Composers

Includes Streaming Videos!

Damon Ferrante

Book, Streaming Videos & MP3 Audio

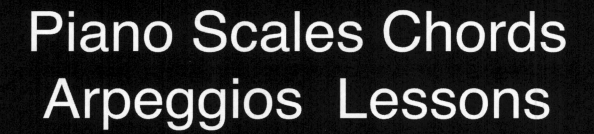

Piano Scales Chords
Arpeggios Lessons

Book & Videos   Damon Ferrante

Guitar Book
for Kids 5 & Up

by Damon Ferrante

No Music Reading Required

- Beginner Lessons -
Book & Streaming Videos